Lizard over Ice

Gervase Phinn

Nelson

Thomas Nelson and Sons Ltd
Nelson House Mayfield Road
Walton-on-Thames Surrey
KT12 5PL UK

Thomas Nelson Australia
102 Dodds Street
South Melbourne
Victoria 3205 Australia

Nelson Canada
1120 Birchmount Road
Scarborough Ontario
M1K 5G4 Canada

© **Gervase Phinn**

First published by Thomas Nelson and Sons Ltd 1990

I(T)P   Thomas Nelson is an International
        Thomson Publishing Company

I(T)P   is used under licence

ISBN 0-17-439211-7
NPN 9 8 7 6 5 4

Cover illustration: Sue Hillwood-Harris
Illustrations: Peter Bailey, Judy Brown, Celia Canning,
Richard Crawford, Sian Davies, Toni Goffe, Pauline King,
Kaoru Miyake, Tony Morris, Alan Rowe, Martin Salisbury,
David Eaton and Joe Wright.
Series Design by Richard Crawford

Printed in China

Contents

Contents

Contents

Contents

Acknowledgements

The editor and publishers are grateful to the following for permission to reproduce copyright material:

HILAIRE BELLOC 'Henry King' reprinted by permission of Duckworth and Company Ltd; CHRISTINE BENTLEY 'A Special Brew', 'Alphabet of Love', 'Downpour' and 'Eight Epitaphs' used by permission of the author; CAREY BLYTON 'Night Starvation, or The Biter Bit' reprinted by permission of Carey Blyton, composer/author; MOLLY BROWN 'Lizzi's Lament' used by permission of the author; CAROL COIFFAIT 'Who is he?' used by permission of the author; WENDY COPE 'Kenneth' reprinted by permission of Faber and Faber Ltd from uncollected poems by Wendy Cope; JOHN COTTON 'A Week to Christmas' and 'Our Alphabetical Class' used by permission of the author; JOHN CUNLIFFE 'Crab', 'I like to sit', 'A city of thousands', 'The Ballad of Johnny Shiner', 'An Urgent Call to the Dentist', 'Epitaphs on a Bus Conductor and a Weaver' and 'Asleep' from *Standing on a Strawberry* reprinted by permission of Andre Deutsch; BERLIE DOHERTY 'White Water', 'Contrasts' and 'Mars to Earth' reprinted by permission of the author; SERGEI ESENIN 'Night', translated by Geoffrey Thurley, from *Confessions of a Hooligan*, reprinted by permission of Carcanet Press Ltd; MAX FATCHEN 'Growing', from *Songs for my Dog and Other People* (Kestrel Books 1980) © Max Fatchen 1980, reprinted by permission of Penguin Books Ltd; VICKI FEAVER 'Latch-key Child' is reprinted by permission of Martin Secker and Warburg Ltd; ROY FULLER 'A schoolmistress called Binks...' and 'Here lies a greedy girl' used by permission of the author; PAMELA GILLIAN 'Invasion' used by permission of the author; MICK GOWER 'Christmas Thank-yous' from *Swings and Roundabouts* is reprinted by permission of William Collins and Sons Ltd; WILLIAM HART-SMITH 'The Beach' and 'Razor Fish' reproduced from *Selected Poems of William Hart-Smith* by kind permission of Angus & Robertson (UK) Ltd; SUE HASTEAD 'Space for Both of Us' used by permission of the author; LANGSTON HUGHES 'Mother to Son' reprinted by permission of Aitken and Stone Ltd; KARLA KUSKIN 'Cow' from *Near the Window Tree: Poems by Karla Kuskin* © 1975 by Karla Kuskin reprinted by permission of Harper & Row, Publishers, Inc; PHILIP LARKIN 'Take one Home for the Kiddies' reprinted by permission of Faber & Faber Ltd; D.H. LAWRENCE 'Little Fish' is reprinted by permission of Laurence Pollinger Ltd. and the estate of Mrs. Frieda Lawrence Ravagli; DENNIS LEE 'Curse' reproduced from *Nicholas Knock and Other People*, published by Macmillan of Canada © Dennis Lee; WES MAGEE 'The House on the Hill', 'Up on the Downs', 'The Witche's Brew', 'On Monday Morning', 'The Game... at the Hallowe'en Party' and 'An Accident' used by kind permission of the author; ROGER MCGOUGH 'Watchwords' and 'The Allivator' from *Watchwords* reprinted by permission of Jonathan Cape Ltd; GERARD MELIA 'Names in Stone' and 'Follow Daniel' reprinted by permission of the author; EVE MERRIAM 'Ping-Pong' from *Pudmuddle Jump In* (ed. Beverley Mathias) reprinted by permission of Methuen Children's Books; TATSUJI MYOSHI 'The Ground' from *An Anthology of Modern Japanese Poetry* (eds. I. Kono and R. Fukada) reprinted by permission of Kenkyusha Ltd; JOHN MOLE 'Mr Cartwright's Counting Rhyme', 'Who, Sir, am I?' and 'I am the shame beneath the carpet' from *Boo to a Goose* (Peterloo Poets 1987) reprinted by permission of the author; OGDEN NASH 'The Duck', produced by permission of Curtis Brown, London, on behalf of the Estate of Ogden Nash; JUDITH NICHOLLS 'Season Song', 'Wolf', 'Tiger', 'Bully', 'December' and 'Storytime' from *Midnight Forest* reprinted by permission of Faber & Faber Ltd; GARETH OWEN 'Cycling down the Street...' and 'Conversation Piece' © Gareth Owen reprinted by permission of the author; GERVASE PHINN 'Yeti', 'Phamily Phantoms', 'The Nokk' and 'Dear Teacher' used by permission of the author; JOHN RICE 'Seaside Song' used by permission of the author; IAN SERRAILLIER 'Spell To Find a Lost Season Ticket' from *I'll Tell You A Tale* is reprinted by permission of Longman and Puffin Books; J.R.R. TOLKIEN 'Oliphaunt', an extract from *The adventures of Tom Bombadil*, reproduced by kind permission of Unwin

Acknowledgements

Hyman Ltd; TRADITIONAL 'A Little Yellow Cricket' from *Papago Indians of South Arizona* by Ruth Murray Underhill reprinted by permission of University of California Press; COLIN WEST 'Allow me to describe myself' from *Pudmuddle Jump In* (ed. Beverley Mathias) reprinted by permission of Methuen Cildren's Books; W.B. YEATS 'The Stolen Child' reprinted by permission of A.P. Watt Ltd on behalf of Michael B. Yeats and Macmillan London Ltd; CHARLOTTE ZOLOTOW 'Scene' from *River Winding* reprinted by permission of Blackie and Son Ltd.

The editor wishes to thank his former pupils for permission to include their poems in this anthology.

Every effort has been made to trace copyright holders and to make appropriate acknowledgements. The publishers would be pleased to hear from authors whose work appears without acknowledgement and to whom a fee may be due.

With thanks to Sue Hasted.

Introduction

'Poetry needs to be at the heart of work in English because of the quality of language at work on experience that it offers to us. If language becomes separated from moral and emotional life - becomes merely a trail of cliches which neither communicate with nor quicken the mind of the reader - then we run the risk of depriving children of the kind of vital resource of language which poetry provides.'

Teaching Poetry in the Secondary School: An HMI view.

The passage above is quoted in *English for ages 5 to 16*, the national curriculum document, which also states that 'poetry needs to be a central part of the reading programmes throughout the secondary sector' and that 'it is crucial that teachers' attitudes to poetry communicate enthusiasm for it'. Poetry is now named as an essential element in the attainment targets for Levels 3 and above. Pupils are expected to begin to read poetry, aloud or silently, and talk about their preferences for particular poems, eventually even writing about them at Level 5. Poetry cannot be avoided any longer!

Yet over the years poetry has always been the poor relation of fiction in the classroom. The Assessment of Performance Unit's Secondary Survey *Language Performance in Schools* reported that many children disliked poetry, considering it difficult and demanding and largely irrelevant to their lives and interests. Earlier, the Bullock Report (*A Language for Life*, 1975) noted that 'in many schools [poetry] suffers from lack of commitment, misunderstanding, and the wrong kind of orientation: above all, it lacks adequate resources'. It seems clear that teachers did not like teaching poetry, and pupils did not like having it taught to them. Have times changed? Not enough, we fear.

The Nelson poetry anthology, *Lizard over Ice*, aims to alleviate some of the continuing uncertainty about how to handle poetry in the classroom. It takes poetry firmly out of the ivory tower and helps children to see that poets are people like themselves, speaking to other people about common human experience, but in words that make such experience come alive.

Melvyn Bragg, in his introduction to *How to Enjoy Poetry* by Vernon Scannell, says

'Poetry is a most wonderful art: to read, to listen to, to attempt. It takes the gift of language and pays it the respect of fashioning it into the finest forms while retaining a grip on the human measure of life. For many, it is dinned into

their unwilling heads at school, trailed across their noses in restless adolescence and ever after considered as part of "another" world. Yet the real world has been the poet's prime concern. And many of us believe that the real world has been represented more accurately and powerfully by poets than by anyone else.'

Lizard over Ice is not for dinning into unwilling heads; it hopes to make poetry a participatory activity, offering children a chance to respond to vivid use of language and to experiment with different ways to express their own feelings and perceptions in language. It contains over 150 exciting and largely unfamiliar poems. There are haiku, jokes and riddles, shape poems, chants and charms and magic words. There are poems to surprise and please, to make you think or make you laugh, to perform aloud or read alone. There are rhymes and ballads and strong rhythms, solemn, stately lyrics and silly limericks. They come from Europe and Africa, and Caribbean and the Far East, Australia and America - and some are the work of children themselves.

The anthology is divided into fifteen sections so you can find your way about easily, although there are many other ways in which the poems could be combined. Each section is followed by ideas for discussion and starting points and strategies for pupils' own writing, encouraging children to enjoy and appreciate poetry - and to think of themselves as poets too.

Miniatures

Poets are painters with words. They put down on paper the pictures or images which come into their mind. Some poets not only describe the shape and colour, taste and smell of things, but they also try to capture their own moods and feelings.

Poets use words in a special way. They try to make their readers or listeners feel as closely as possible to the way they feel about the person or scene or whatever they are writing about.

Like a painter, a poet looks very carefully at the subject. Then he or she chooses the best words to describe it. Sometimes the poems will be long and detailed and at other times short and vivid. The poems in this section are all miniature word pictures where the poets try to capture exactly, in just a few lines, an image of the sea or the stars, a yellow cricket or a pig, a cow or a tiny fish, fog or dusk or thunder.

Snapshot

The gutter is edged with diamonds
the birds are drinking them.

Pierre Reverdy

The Ground

Ants
are dragging a wing of a butterfly
See!
it is like a yacht.

Tatsuji Miyoshi
Japan
Translated by I.Kono

Fog

The fog comes
on little cat feet.
It sits looking
over harbor and city
on silent haunches
and then moves on.

Carl Sandburg
United States

Dusk

Butterfly, blinded
by smoke, drifts like torn paper
to the flames below.

Judith Nicholls
Britain

Thunder

I hear
the drummers
strike
the sky.

Glenys Van Every
Britain

A Little Yellow Cricket

A little yellow cricket
At the roots of the corn
Is hopping about and singing.

Traditional Papago
(Native American)

Cow

'Cow' sounds heavy.
Cow
Standing in the meadow
Chewing.
A big fur box on legs
Mooing.

Karla Kuskin
United States

Pig

With sun on his back and sun on his belly,
His head as big and unmoving
As a cannon,
The pig is working.

Paul Eluard
France

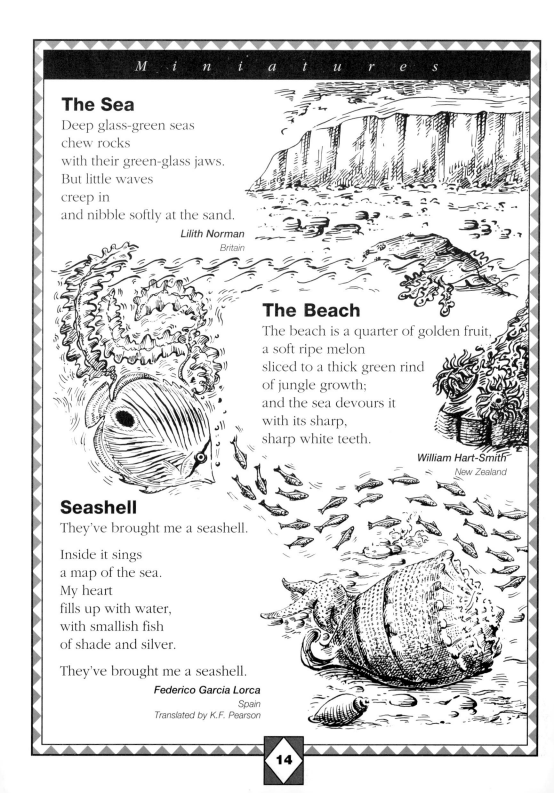

The Sea

Deep glass-green seas
chew rocks
with their green-glass jaws.
But little waves
creep in
and nibble softly at the sand.

Lilith Norman
Britain

The Beach

The beach is a quarter of golden fruit,
a soft ripe melon
sliced to a thick green rind
of jungle growth;
and the sea devours it
with its sharp,
sharp white teeth.

William Hart-Smith
New Zealand

Seashell

They've brought me a seashell.

Inside it sings
a map of the sea.
My heart
fills up with water,
with smallish fish
of shade and silver.

They've brought me a seashell.

Federico Garcia Lorca
Spain
Translated by K.F. Pearson

14

Little Fish

The tiny fish enjoy themselves
in the sea.
Quick little splinters of life,
their little lives are fun to them
in the sea.

D.H. Lawrence
Britain

Jellyfish

Floating plate of misted glass
With swollen purple belly.
Tentacles of waving grass
A living pumping jelly.

Sandra Convey, age 13

Song: The Railway Train

You see the smoke at Kapunda
The steam puffs regularly,
Showing quickly, it looks like frost,
It runs like running water,
It blows like a spouting whale.

Traditional Narranyeri
(Australian Aboriginal)
Translated by G. Taplin

Season Song

Spring stirs slowly, shuffles, hops;
Summer dances close behind.
Autumn is a jostling crowd
but Winter creeps into your mind.

Judith Nicholls
Britain

Stars

Near the book a notebook
near the notebook a glass
near the glass a child
in the child's hand a cat.
And far away stars stars.

Oktay Rifat
Turkey
Translated by K. Bosley

The Viking Terror

There's a wicked wind tonight,
Wild upheaval in the sea;
No fear now that the Viking hordes
Will terrify me.

Traditional Gaelic
Translated by Brendan Kennelly

Scene

Little trees like pencil strokes
black and still
etched forever in my mind
on that snowy hill.

Charlotte Zolotow
United States

Follow-on

Write your own miniature poem using just a few lines.

- Decide on a subject. It could be:

  a person - old man, clown, tramp, boxer
  a season or month
  a festival - Christmas, Eid or Durga for example
  an event - birthday party, football match, pantomime
  a disaster - earthquake, fire, flood
  a mood - anger, fear, boredom
  or anything you choose.

- Jot down any words or phrases about your chosen subject.

- From your notes, decide on one clear image which creates a picture in miniature of the subject. You might, like some of the poets you have come across in this selection, use similes and metaphors to create a vivid and interesting picture.

Simile

In the poem *Pig*, Paul Eluard compares the animal's head to a cannon:

'His head *as* big and unmoving *as* a cannon'.

In *Song*, the poet compares the steam from the train to several things:

'... It looks *like* frost
It runs *like* running water
It blows *like* a spouting whale'.

Both poets are using similes. This is where we say that something is like, or very similar to, something else.

Metaphor

In *Little Fish*, D.H. Lawrence compares the fish with 'quick little splinters of life' without using the words 'like' or 'as'. He says that something *is* something else - that the fish *are* splinters.

We know that in reality fish are not really splinters, but the idea gives us a very exact and unusual image. This kind of image is called a metaphor.

Lilith Norman in *The Sea* uses a very striking and colourful metaphor:

'Deep glass-green seas

Chew rocks

with their green-glass jaws.'

- Write a first draft of your poem. Do not try to make it rhyme. Keep to three or four lines.

- Let someone else read your poem and give suggestions on how he or she feels it could be improved.

- Write out your final draft. You might like to illustrate your poem.

Haiku

A miniature picture in words which follows a fixed pattern is the haiku. This is traditionally a Japanese seasonal poem and is usually written as seventeen syllables, and it consists of only three lines:

- the first of five syllables
- the second of seven syllables
- the third of five syllables.

The first line sets the scene, the second line introduces some action and the third line 'fuses' the two; that is, it brings them together. Kenneth Koch writes that in a haiku 'it is as if a beautiful, brief moment is being seen in slow motion'.

Wolf

still on his lone rock
stares at the uncaged stars and
cries into the night.

Judith Nicholls
Britain

Seasonal Haiku

Buds full, fat and green
Pink blossoms trembling on trees.
The warm breath of SPRING.

A burnished brass face
In an empty, cloudless sky
Smiles with SUMMER heat.

Curled and twisted leaves
Carpet red the cold dead earth.
AUTUMN'S withered hand.

Bitter winds of ice
Brittle grass like icy spikes.
Old soldier WINTER.

Richard Matthews, age 17

I like the sound of rain

I like the sound
of rain; how I long to hear
the sound of dew!

With the first rain
the snails come out to roam
like children at a fiesta.

Anton Buttigieg
Malta
Translated by F. Ebejer

Mark

Hair a tangled mop
Broken teeth and runny nose -
That's my brother Mark.

Helen White, age 11

A bitter morning

A bitter morning,
sparrows sitting together
without any necks.

Anonymous
Japan
Translated by J.W. Hackett

White Water

White water. Canoes
Flip, frail as winter twigs, down
to black river calm.

Across still water
Voices, light laughter, singing
Drift like distant dreams.

Heavy heron flies
Head-tucked, slow-winged, sleep-grey, calm.
Lands, and turns to stone.

Did you see the moon
Stealthy as foxes, slip down
To the forest clouds?

Berlie Doherty
Britain

Friend

Oh, farewell false friend!
I shared with you my secrets,
Which you shared with all.

Bernadette Scanlon, age 16

Tiger

Tiger, eyes dark with
half-remembered forest night,
stalks an empty cage.

Judith Nicholls
Britain

Haiku Haiku

hai-ku
      hai-ku
           hai-
coo the pigeons   in springtime
                                     -ku
                                        hai-ku
                                            hai-ku

Adrian Henri
Britain

Follow-on

Try writing some haiku yourself. Your short poems could be about the different times of year, but they could also be about:

    moods - happiness, anger, fear

    animals, insects or fish

    people - baby, wrestler, jogger, old man or woman

    places - seaside, farmyard, motorway, cathedral.

Now you have tried your hand at writing miniature poems and haiku you are ready to tackle something longer and more adventurous.

A good way to start is by using other poets as models for your writing. You can get ideas for your own poems from reading them, and imitate their different styles and structures.

When he was a boy one of the greatest English poets, Alexander Pope, imitated the poems of earlier and very famous writers like Chaucer and Spenser. Another great poet, John Keats, made imitations of Shakespeare and Milton when he was young, before deciding on his own individual style of writing.

Some of the pupils' poems in this section are based on the work of professional writers.

I Am Black

I am black as I thought
My lids are as brown as
I thought
My hair is curled as I
thought
I am free as I know.

Accabre Huntley
Britain

I Am

I am small for my age: Hi Titch!
Thin as a beanpole: Oi Skinny!
I wear glasses and get spots:
Look at spotty four eyes!
I always come top in maths:
Listen to the Professor!
I am me: I can't help it!

Anonymous
Britain

Night

Silently sleeps the river.
The dark pines hold their peace.
The nightingale does not sing,
Or the corncrake screech.

Night. Silence enfolds.
Only the brook murmurs,
And the brilliant moon turns
Everything to silver.

Silver the river,
And the rivulets.
Silver the grass
Of the fertile steppes.

Night. Silence enfolds.
All sleeps in Nature
And the brilliant moon
Turns everything to silver.

Sergei Esenin
Soviet Union
Translated by G. Thurley

Night

Gently laps the sea.
The black rocks glisten wet.
Moonlight silvers the sand,
And the gulls are quiet.

Night. Ice in the air.
Trees silhouetted, stark, straight.
Branches like ragged birds.
So still, so black.

Beyond the dark rocks -
Stretching shingle to the sea.
Patches of blue mud
And pools of silver.

Night. Ice in the water.
Great Neptune sleeps
And in the cold, cold deep,
All is still, all is black.

Richard Pasco, age 15

In the Stump of the Old Tree

In the stump of the old tree, where the heart has rotted out,/there is a
hole the length of a man's arm, and a dank pool at the/bottom of it
where the rain gathers, and the old leaves turn into/lacy skeletons. But
do not put your hand down to see, because

in the stumps of old trees, where the hearts have rotted out,/there are
holes the length of a man's arm, and dank pools at the/bottom where
the rain gathers and old leaves turn to lace, and the/beak of a dead
bird gapes like a trap. But do not put your/hand down to see, because

in the stumps of old trees with rotten hearts, where the rain/gathers
and the laced leaves and the dead bird like a trap, there/are holes the
length of a man's arm, and in every crevice of the/rotten wood grow
weasels' eyes like molluscs, their lids open and shut with the tide. But
do not put your hand down to see, because

in the stumps of old trees where the rain gathers and the/trapped
leaves and the beak, and the laced weasel's eyes, there are holes the
length of a man's arm, and at the bottom a sodden bible/written in the
language of rooks. But do not put your hand down/to see because

in the stumps of old trees where the hearts have rotted out there are
holes the length of a man's arm where the weasels are/trapped and the
letters of the rook language are laced on the sodden leaves, and at the
bottom there is a man's arm. But do/not put your hand down to see
because

in the stumps of old trees where the hearts have rotted out/there are
deep holes and dank pools where the rain gathers, and/if you ever put
your hand down to see, you can wipe it in the/sharp grass till it bleeds,
but you'll never want to eat with/it again.

Hugh Sykes-Davies
Britain

26

The Tree Stump

In the stump of the old tree,
Where the maggots lurk in the darkness,
And the carcase of an ancient rook rots in rigid death,
And shadows shudder,
The devil breathes,
But do not look inside because ...

In the stump of the old tree,
Where the dark maggots lurk on the carcase of an ancient rook,
Where the devil's breath shivers the shadows,
A golden guinea gleams from a crevice,
But do not look inside because ...

In the stump of the old tree,
Where lurking maggots creep in the carcase of an ancient rook,
A breathing devil haunts the darkness,
With golden eyes like gleaming guineas,
And waits for one curious pair of eyes,
But do not look inside because ...

In the stump of the old tree,
Where maggots slither in the carcase,
in the breathing darkness,
The gleaming devil's eyes close upon
The curious
And they'll never see again!

Richard Jeffars, age 12

Polar Bear

I saw a polar bear
on an ice-drift.
He seemed harmless as a dog,
who comes running towards you,
wagging his tail.
But so much
did he want to get at me
that when I jumped aside
he went spinning on the ice.
We played this game of tag
from morning until dusk.
But then at last, I tired him out,
and ran my spear into his side.

Anonymous
Iglukik Eskimo (Canada)
Translated by T. Lowenstein

Dog

I saw this huge dog
behind the gate.
He slavered and snarled
And growled, watching, waiting.
His tail was like a thick rope
And his black bristly hair like a mat.
'He won't hurt you lovey',
Said the old woman from the door.
I threw her paper up the path,
And ran!

Paul Calladine, age 13

What is Red?

Red is a sunset
Blazing and bright.
Red is feeling brave
With all your might.
Red is a sunburn
Spot on your nose.
Sometimes red
Is a red, red rose.
Red squiggles out
When you cut your hand.
Red is a brick and
The sound of a band.
Red is a hotness
You get inside
When you're embarrassed
And want to hide.
Firecracker, fire-engine
Fire-flicker red -
And when you're angry
Red runs through your head.
Red is an Indian,
A valentine heart,
The trimming on
A circus cart.

Red is a lipstick,
Red is a shout,
Red is a signal
That says: 'Watch out!'
Red is a great big
Rubber ball.
Red is the giant-est
Colour of all.
Red is a show-off
No doubt about it -
But can you imagine
Living without it?

Mary O'Neill

Black is the Color

Black is the color of my true love's skin
Black is the color of his twin
Black is the color of my true love's hair
Black is the color of berries sweet and wild
Black is the color of gems most rare
Black is the color of my favourite child.

Ruth Duckett Gibbs
United States

Bully

Slowly he straightened his back,
ran chewed stumps through his hair;

slowly he straightened leathered knees
and got up from his chair.

Slowly he fixed me with his eye
(I dared not leave his glare);

slowly he reached to his pocket,
put something there.

Slowly he stepped towards me,
his mouth curled in a grin;

slowly, slowly, he came closer ...
Quickly ... I RAN!

Judith Nicholls
Britain

Bully

I hated him.
Everyone hated him
Dark brown glassy snake-eyed
Searching everyone, everything.
Long, slit of a mouth
Above a sharp chin.
Boots worn down
Trousers frayed and holed at the knee
Shirt with a dirty collar,
A bully of all bullies.

Matthew Delaney, age 12

Thief

Quickly she glanced from left to right,
Curving her body;

Quickly she opened her bag wide,
Like the jaws of a shark;

Quickly she tipped the tin forward.
The jaws snapped shut;

Quickly she scurried for the door,
Looking dead ahead;

Quickly, quickly the store detective pounced.
Slowly ... she sighed.

Pat Williams, age 13

Contrasts

On white snow
black crows
flap
Torn scraps

Yellow daffodils
blaze
like cupped suns
in their
wet green skies
of grass

Clouds
grey with sullen rain
let sudden blue through
like a promise

October red sun
flares
over brown earth
showering orange fire

Berlie Doherty
Britain

Who is he?

I saw him again
In the wind and rain
Dog on a string
A bagfull of things
Blue tattoos
Worn out shoes
Flapping coat
Scarf at throat
Angry brows
And no one knows
Who he is
Or where
He goes!

Carol Coiffait
Britain

Follow-on

In small groups, look at one pair of poems from the following:

Night by Sergei Esenin
Night by Richard Pasco

In the Stump of the Old Tree by Hugh Sykes-Davies
The Tree Stump by Richard Jeffars

Polar Bear by T. Lowenstein
Dog by Paul Calladine

I Am Black by Accabre Huntley
I Am (Anonymous)

• Discuss the similarities and differences. Use the following headings as a guide:

Subject - are they both about the same thing?

Mood - are they both funny or sad or gloomy or bright?

Clarity - are there any parts you don't understand?

Words and phrases - compare these.

Structure - think about such things as verses and line length.

Images - the word pictures that are used, metaphors and similes.

Rhymes - do both poems use the same rhymes?

Which of the two poems do you prefer? Say why.

• Write a poem of your own using a poem in this section as a model. It might be a poem based on the two you have discussed, or it might be based on one of the other poems in the section.

Rhyme is when two words sound alike. Sometimes poets use rhyme to get our attention, or to make us listen, or to create a pleasing musical effect. Rhyme can also give pattern to the verses in a poem.

In most rhyming poems the rhyme appears at the end of the line, as in the first verse of this poem I wrote:

Nightmare Noises

On a clifftop perched up high,
Underneath a blood-red sky,
A gloomy, grim-walled castle stands.
Its turrets rise like great grey hands
And windows stare like sightless eyes
And echoing round the walls are cries
Of creatures long since dead.

Sometimes a rhyme might appear in the middle of a line, as in another of my poems:

Classroom Creatures

Mrs Price, isn't nice
Her tiger eyes burn like ice.
Mr Ryan, hard as iron
Stalks the classroom like a lion.
Mrs Drew, little shrew
Very nervous, very new.
Mr Ash, walrus 'tash,
Brings us all out in a rash.
Mrs Page, in a rage,
Is like an elephant in a cage.
Mr Brass, silly ass,
Plays the fool in every class
But Mrs Meacher, the Headteacher
Is the most unpleasant creature.

Full rhyme 'High' and 'sky', 'shrew' and 'new' are full rhymes, where the words sound exactly alike.

Near or half rhyme In my next poem 'mine' and 'grime' are very similar in sound but they are not full rhymes. These are called near rhymes or half rhymes.

Miner

Like some great stooping monster
He emerges from the mine.
His red eyes ringed with coal dust
And his black hair thick with grime.
He pauses by the pit-head
As the others walk on by
And wipes the sweat from his face of jet
And smiles at the cloudless sky.

Quatrains The following four poems are quatrains, verses of four lines, but I have used different rhyming forms:

I got this gift from Auntie Netta	*A*
So I wrote to her this letter:	*A*
'Thank you for the super sweater	*A*
But on the sheep it looked much better!'	*A*

When Dracula met his future bride,	*A*
Did she languish by his side,	*A*
And on that dark, romantic night,	*B*
Was it true love at first bite?	*B*

'Thank you doctor for your concern,'	*A*
He said with fevered brow,	*B*
'I used to be a were-wolf,	*C*
But I'm all right nooooowwwwww !!'	*B*

Said one theatre ghost to another one day :	*A*
'When I was in my prime,	*B*
I acted in every sort of play,	*A*
Now I just do phantomime!'	*B*

You will notice a real range of rhyming patterns in this section.

Things

Trains are for going,
Boats are for rowing,
Seeds are for sowing,
Noses for blowing,
And sleeping's for bed.

Dogs are for pawing.
Logs are for sawing,
Crows are for cawing,
Rivers for thawing,
And sleeping's for bed.

Flags are for flying,
Stores are for buying,
Glasses for spying,
Babies for crying,
And sleeping's for bed.

Cows are for mooing,
Chickens for shooing,
Blue is for bluing,
Things are for doing,
And sleeping's for bed.

Games are for playing,
Hay is for haying,
Horses for neighing,
Saying's for saying,
And sleeping's for bed.

Money's for spending,
Patients for tending,
Branches for bending;
Poems for ending,
And sleeping's for bed.

William Jay Smith

The Duck

Behold the duck.
It does not cluck.
A cluck it lacks.
It quacks.
It is especially fond
Of a puddle or a pond.
When it dines or sups,
It bottom ups.

Ogden Nash
Britain

Take one Home for the Kiddies

On shallow straw, in shadeless glass,
Huddled by empty bowls, they sleep:
No dark, no dam, no earth, no grass -
Mam, get us one of them to keep.

Living toys are something novel,
But it soon wears off somehow.
Fetch the shoebox, fetch the shovel -
Mam, we're playing funerals now.

Philip Larkin
Britain

Oliphaunt

Grey as a mouse,
Big as a house,
Nose like a snake,
I make the earth shake,
As I tramp through the grass;
Trees crack as I pass.
With horns in my mouth
I walk in the South,
Flapping big ears.
Beyond count of years
I stump round and round,
Never lie on the ground,
Not even to die.
Oliphaunt am I,
Biggest of all,
Huge, old, and tall.
If ever you'd met me,
You wouldn't forget me.
If you never do,
You won't think I'm true;
But old Oliphaunt am I,
And I never lie.

J.R.R. Tolkien
Britain

Wolves!

Wolves! Wolves! Everywhere!
This is their place,
This is their territory,
Where they rule supreme.
Dark packs - lone tracks -
Grey shapes, long tongues,
Noses high in the air
Smelling blood!
Don't dare! Don't dare!
Enter their place,
Or like the stray stag
You'll never return there.

Craig Roberts, age 13

A Week to Christmas

Sunday with six whole days to go.
How we'll endure it I don't know!

Monday the goodies are in the
    making,
Spice smells of pudding and mince
    pies a-baking.

Tuesday, Dad's home late and quiet
    as a mouse
He smuggles packages into the house.

Wednesday's the day for decorating
    the tree,
Will the lights work again? We'll have
    to see!

Thursday's for last minute shopping
    and hurry,
We've never seen Mum in quite such
    a flurry!

Friday is Christmas Eve when we'll lie
    awake
Trying to sleep before the day break

And that special quiet of Christmas
    morn
When out there somewhere Christ
    was born.

John Cotton
Britain

Lizzi's Lament

My life is in a tizzi
My hair is always frizzi
My head is feeling dizzi
My stomach's kinda wizzi.

Try to talk to people
But they're so bizzi

If God ain't in Heaven,
Where izzi?

Who knows,
I think I'm going crizzi.

Molly Brown
Ireland

Mr Cartwright's Counting Rhyme

One, two
You, boy, yes I'm talking to you

three, four
I've wiped the floor

five, six
with others of your kind. Your tricks

seven, eight
come centuries too late

nine, ten
for experienced men

eleven, twelve
like myself

thirteen, fourteen
so just be careful to be more seen

fifteen, sixteen
than heard, or preferably not seen

seventeen, eighteen
at all. Or you could stop baiting

nineteen, twenty
and pity me.

John Mole
Britain

The House on the Hill

It was built years ago
by someone quite manic
and sends those who go there
away in blind panic.
They tell tales of horrors
that can injure or kill
designed by the madman
who lived on the hill.

If you visit the House on the Hill for a dare
remember my words ... 'There are dangers. Beware!'

The piano's white teeth
when you plonk out a note
will bite off your fingers
then reach for your throat.
The living room curtains
- long, heavy and black -
will wrap you in cobwebs
if you're slow to step back.

If you enter the House on the Hill for a dare
remember my words ... 'There are dangers. Beware!'

The 'fridge in the kitchen
has a self-closing door.
If it knocks you inside
then you're ice cubes ... for sure.
The steps to the cellar
are littered with bones,
and up from the darkness
drift creakings and groans.

If you go to the House on the Hill for a dare
remember my words ... 'There are dangers. Beware!'

Turn on the hot tap
and the bathroom will flood
not with gallons of water
but litres of blood.
The rocking-chair's arms
can squeeze you to death;
a waste of time shouting
as you run ... out ... of ... breath.

Don't say you weren't warned or told to take care
when you entered the House on the Hill ... for a dare.

Wes Magee
Britain

Names in Stone

Dead and lying neath the stones
Nussey, Hough and Sally Jones;
Fordham, Bently, Monsieur Boughe
Willow herb and candy tuft.

Churchyard flies and pollen seed
Trapeze around the railway weed
Daisy Trotti, a treasured maid
Dandelion, skutch grass, yellowed braid.

Butterfly, and wild red rose
Tolson, Coatsworth, Tom Melrose
Waiting for eternal dawn,
Spetch, Ormeroyd, General Vaughan.

(All names found on gravestones in Wooley
Churchyard, Yorkshire, July 1985)

Gerard Melia
Britain

Jamaica market

Honey, pepper, leaf-green limes,
Pagan fruit whose names are rhymes,
Mangoes, breadfruit, ginger-roots,
Granadillas, bamboo-shoots,
Cho-cho, ackees, tangerines,
Lemons, purple Congo-beans,
Sugar, okras, kola-nuts,
Citrons, hairy coconuts,
Fish, tobacco, native hats,
Gold bananas, woven mats,
Plantains, wild-thyme, pallid leeks,
Pigeons with their scarlet beaks,
Oranges and saffron yams,
Baskets, ruby guava jams,
Turtles, goat-skins, cinnamon,
Allspice, conch-shells, golden rum.
Black skins, babel and the sun
That burns all colours into one.

Agnes Maxwell-Hall
Jamaica

Follow-on

• Make a small collection of rhyming poems you have enjoyed reading which have different rhyming forms.

• In a group, see how many rhymes you know - nursery rhymes, playground rhymes, jingles, football chants, song lyrics, dialect poems. Can you remember when you learned these rhymes and who taught you?

• Try writing a rhyming couplet or a quatrain about
an eel, shark or whale
a lion, wolf or mouse
a fire, wind or storm
a beach, the sea, a wood
a general, a queen, someone or something you know well.

All poems have a rhythm, that is, a pattern of beats or sounds. Some poems have a slow, stately rhythm, others a regular, sing-song rhythm. The poems in this section have a strong, lively, invigorating rhythm to set your feet tapping.

Seaside song

It was a
sunboiled brightlight friedegg hotskin suntanned
sizzler of a day

It was a
popsong dingdong candyfloss dodgemcar
    spaceinvader beachwader
smashing seaside town

We had a
swelltime a welltime a realpellmelltime
a finetime a rhymetime a superdoubledimetime

We beachswam ate ham gobbledup a chicken leg
climbed trees chased bees
got stuck in mud up to our knees
played chase flew in space
beat a seagull in a skating race
rowed boats quenched throats
spent a load of £5 notes
sang songs hummed tunes
played hide-and-seek in sandy dunes
did all these things, too much by far,
that we fell asleep going back in the car ...
from Folkestone.

John Rice
Britain

Daniel

(Inscribed to Isador Bennett Reed)

Darius the Mede was a king and a wonder.
His eye was proud, and his voice was thunder.
He kept bad lions in a monstrous den.
He fed up the lions on Christian men.
Daniel was the chief hired man of the land.
He stirred up the jazz in the palace band.
He whitewashed the cellar. He shovelled in the coal.
And Daniel kept a-praying 'Lord save my soul.'
Daniel kept a-praying 'Lord save my soul.'
Daniel kept a-praying 'Lord save my soul.'

Daniel was the butler, swagger and swell.
He ran up stairs. He answered the bell.
And he would let in whoever came a-calling -
Saints so holy, scamps so appalling.
'Old man Ahab leaves his card.
Elisha and the bears are a-waiting in the yard.
Here comes Pharaoh and his snakes a-calling.
Here comes Cain and his wife a-calling.
Shadrach, Meshach and Abednego for tea.
Here comes Jonah and the whale,
And the Sea!
Here comes St Peter and his fishing pole.
Here comes Judas and his silver a-calling.
Here comes old Beelzebub a-calling.'
And Daniel kept a-praying 'Lord save my soul.'
Daniel kept a-praying 'Lord save my soul.'
Daniel kept a-praying 'Lord save my soul.'

His sweetheart and his mother were Christian and meek.
They washed and ironed for Darius every week.
One Thursday he met them at the door -
Paid them as usual, but acted sore.

He said 'Your Daniel is a dead little pigeon.
He's a good hard worker, but he talks religion.'
And he showed them Daniel in the lions' cage.
Daniel standing quietly, the lions in a rage.
His good old mother cried 'Lord save him.'
And Daniel's tender sweetheart cried 'Lord save him.'

Beginning with a strain of
'Dixie'.

With a touch of
'Alexander's Band'.

And she was a golden lily in the dew.
And she was as sweet as an apple on the tree,
And she was as fine as a melon in the corn-field,
Gliding and lovely as a ship on the sea,
Gliding and lovely as a ship on the sea.

And she prayed to the Lord
'Send Gabriel. Send Gabriel.'

King Darius said to the lions
'Bite Daniel. Bite Daniel.
Bite him. Bite him. Bite him!'

Thus roared the lions:
'We want Daniel, Daniel, Daniel,
We want Daniel, Daniel, Daniel.
G rrrrrrrrrrrrrrrrrrrrrrrrrrrrrrrrrrr
G rrrrrrrrrrrrrrrrrrrrrrrrrrrrrrrrrrrr.'

Here the audience roars with the leader.

And Daniel did not frown,
Daniel did not cry.
He kept on looking at the sky
And the Lord said to Gabriel
'Go chain the lions down,
Go chain the lions down,
Go chain the lions down.
Go chain the lions down.'

The audience sings this with the leader, to the tune of the old spiritual.

And Gabriel chained the lions,
And Gabriel chained the lions,
And Gabriel chained the lions,
And Daniel got out of the den,
And Daniel got out of the den,
And Daniel got out of the den.
And Darius said 'You're a Christian child,'
Darius said 'You're a Christian child,'
Darius said 'You're a Christian child,'
And gave him his job again,
And gave him his job again,
And gave him his job again.

Vachel Lindsay

Follow Daniel

Count on Daniel in the shadow,
Lions breath drifts past the grille
Toss a coin, risk his judgement,
Chance a claw against his will.

Feel the press of fear upon you,
Seek his hand; just out of reach.
You're on your own, you've got to risk it,
This is what he has to teach.

Well, I know that that's his way.
I hope they fed the lions today!

Gerard Melia
Britain

Teachers

Teachers shout and bawl at us
Making such a massive fuss.
Homework comes in piles and piles
Essays last for miles and miles.
They give us sums we cannot do
And never think of something new.
The canes they use are ten foot long
And hit you with a great big bong.

Andrew Walsh, age 12

Ping-Pong

Chitchat
wigwag
rick rack
zigzag

Knickknack
geegaw
riffraff
seesaw

crisscross
flip-flop
ding-dong
tiptop

singsong
mishmash
King Kong
bong.

Eve Merriam

Red Boots On

Way down Geneva,
All along Vine,
Deeper than the snow drift
Love's eyes shine:
Mary Lou's walking
In the winter time.

She's got
Red boots on, she's got
Red boots on,
Kicking up the winter
Till the winter's gone.

So

Go by Ontario,
Look down Main,
If you can't find Mary Lou,
Come back again:
Sweet light burning
In winter's flame.

She's got
Snow in her eyes, got
A tingle in her toes
And new red boots on
Wherever she goes

So

All around Lake Street,
Up by St Paul,
Quicker than the white wind
Love takes all:
Mary Lou's walking
In the big snow fall.

She's got
Red boots on, she's got
Red boots on,
Kicking up the winter
Till the winter's gone.

Kit Wright
Britain

Cycling down the Street to meet my Friend John

On my bike and down our street,
Swinging round the bend,
Whizzing past the Library,
Going to meet my friend.

Silver flash of spinning spokes,
Whirr of oily chain,
Bump of tyre on railway line
Just before the train.

The road bends sharp at Pinfold Lane
Like a broken arm,
Brush the branches of the trees
Skirting Batty's Farm.

Tread and gasp and strain and bend
Climbing Gallows' Slope,
Flying down the other side
Like an antelope.

Swanking into Johnnie's street,
Cycling hands on hips,
Past O'Connors corner shop
That always smells of chips.

Bump the door of his backyard
Where we always play,
Lean my bike and knock the door,
'Can John come out to play?'

Gareth Owen
Britain

Up on the Downs

Up on the Downs,
Up on the Downs,
A skylark flutters
And the fox barks shrill,
Brown rabbit scutters
And the hawk hangs still.
Up on the Downs,
Up on the Downs,
With butterflies jigging
like costumed clowns.

Here in the Hills,
Here in the Hills,
The long grass flashes
And the sky seems vast,
Rock lizard dashes
And a crow flies past.
Here in the Hills,
Here in the Hills,
with bumble bees buzzing
like high-speed drills.

High on the Heath,
High on the Heath,
The slow-worm slithers
And the trees are few,
Field-mouse dithers
And the speedwell's blue.
High on the Heath,
High on the Heath,
Where grasshoppers chirp
in the grass beneath.

Wes Magee
Britain

51

Follow-on

Pick one or two of the poems and, in groups, prepare them for performance. You might share out the lines or present them as choral pieces where everyone chants the verses.

Limericks

The poems in this section are limericks: short, amusing and witty verses of five lines. They follow a fixed pattern:

- the first, second and fifth lines rhyme
- the third and fourth lines rhyme
- the first, second and fifth lines have three beats
- the third and fourth lines have two beats.

There was a young lady from Lynn
Who was so excessively thin
That when she assayed
To drink lemonade,
She slipped through the straw
And fell in.

Anonymous

More Limericks by 'Anonymous'

A man on the flying trapeze
Emitted a terrible sneeze.
The consequent force
Shot him right off his course,
And they found him next day in some trees.

There was a young man from Bengal
Who went to a fancy dress ball.
He went just for fun
Dressed up as a bun,
And a dog ate him up in the hall.

There was an old man of Peru,
Who dreamt he was eating his shoe.
He woke in the night
In a terrible fright,
And found it was perfectly true.

There was an old person of Fratton
Who would go to church with his hat on.
'If I wake up,' he said,
'With a hat on my head,
I will know that it hasn't been sat on.'

There was a young lady from Spain
Who was dreadfully sick on a train,
Not once - but again
and again and again
and again and again and again.

There was a young lady from Ickenham
Who went on a bus-trip to Twickenham.
She drank too much beer,
Which made her feel queer,
So she took off her boots and was sick in 'em.

King Midas (or so I am told).
Could turn anything into gold,
From his fork to his knife,
From his son to his wife,
An incredible sight to behold.

Jayne Wilson, age 12

An amazing fast runner called Murray,
Was always in a great hurry,
The reason they say,
Was the trip to Bombay,
Where he sampled a Vindaloo curry.

Andrew Henderson, age 13

There was a young teacher called Phinn
Whose legs were incredibly thin,
When he did the high kicks
They resembled drum sticks
And he played the 'Top Ten' on his chin.

Lesley Calder, age 12

Limericks by Edward Lear

There was an old man of the North
Who fell into a basin of broth;
But a laudable cook
Fished him out with a hook,
Which saved that old man of the North.

There was an old lady of France
Who taught little ducklings to dance;
When she said, 'Tick-a-tack!'
They only said 'Quack!'
Which grieved that old lady of France.

There was an old man with a beard,
Who said, 'It is just as I feared!
Two owls and a hen,
Four larks and a wren,
Have all built their nests in my beard!'

There was a young lady whose chin
Resembled the point of a pin:
So she had it made sharp,
And purchased a harp,
And played several tunes with her chin.

There was an old person of Dover,
Who rushed through a field of blue clover:
But some very large bees
Stung his nose and his knees,
So he very soon went back to Dover.

There was an old man who said, 'How
Shall I flee from that horrible cow?
I will sit on this stile,
And continue to smile,
Which may soften the heart of that cow.'

A Last Word on Limericks, by Anonymous

There was a young man of Japan
Who wrote verse that never would scan.
When they said, 'But the thing
Doesn't go with a a swing',
He said 'Yes, but I always like to get as many words into the last line
    as I possibly can.'

Follow-on

• In groups, tell each other any other limericks you have heard.

• In pairs, write some limericks of your own. Many limericks are about people and often begin with lines like 'There was a young woman from ...' or 'There was an old man of ...'. Yours could be about a person too.

• Read your limericks to others in the class.

• Put all the limericks together in a class anthology entitled something like 'There was a young lady ...'.

Charms, Chants and Magic Words

In this selection are various charms, chants, curses and magic words, some bad and others good, some amusing and others dreadful, which are recited to make things happen.

The Making of a Charm

(*From* Macbeth)
Double, double toil and trouble;
Fire, burn; and, cauldron, bubble.

Fillet of a fenny snake,
In the cauldron boil and bake;
Eye of newt, and toe of frog,
Wool of bat, and tongue of dog,
Adder's fork, and blind-worm's sting,
Lizard's leg, and howlet's wing,
For a charm of powerful trouble,
Like a hell-broth boil and bubble.

Double, double toil and trouble;
Fire, burn; and, cauldron, bubble.

William Shakespeare
Britain

Charm for the Stables

Hang up hooks, and shears to scare
Hence the hag, that rides the mare,
Till they be all over wet,
With the mire, and the sweat:
This observ'd, the manes shall be
Of your horses, all knot-free.

Robert Herrick
Britain

Traveller's Curse After Misdirection

(From the Welsh)

May they stumble, stage by stage
On an endless pilgrimage,
Dawn and dusk, mile after mile,
At each and every step, a stile;
At each and every step withal
May they catch their feet and fall;
At each and every fall they take
May a bone within them break:
And may the bone that breaks within
Not be, for variation's sake,
Now rib, now thigh, now arm, now shin,
But always, without fail, THE NECK.

Robert Graves
Britain

Curse

ON A DRIVER
WHO SPLASHED HIS NEW PANTS
WHEN HE COULD
HAVE JUST AS EASILY
DRIVEN
AROUND THE PUDDLE

May your large intestine freeze in a knot like a skate-lace!
May manhole covers collapse wherever you go.
May garbage strikes pester your street, and may you grow
eight new
Feet and get poison ivy on every toe!

Dennis Lee
Canada

Charm for the Sleeping Child

Let the superstitious wife
Near the child's heart lay a knife:
Point be up, and haft be down;
(While she gossips in the town)
This 'mongst other mystic charms
Keeps the sleeping child from harms.

Robert Herrick
Britain

The Witch's Brew

Into my pot there now must go
Leg of lamb and green frog's toe,

Old men's socks and dirty jeans,
A rotten egg and cold baked beans.

Hubble bubble at the double
Cooking pot stir up some trouble.

One dead fly and a wild wasp's sting,
The eye of a sheep and the heart of a king.

A stolen jewel and mouldy salt,
And for good flavour a jar of malt.
Hubble bubble at the double

Cooking pot stir up some trouble.
Wing of bird and head of mouse,
Screams and howls from a haunted house.

And don't forget the pint of blood,
Or the sardine tin and the clod of mud.

Hubble bubble at the double
Cooking pot stir up some TROUBLE!

Wes Magee
Britain

A Special Brew

Icherty, licherty, fickerty fell
Uchety, buchety, mucherty mell
Brachety, blachety, smacherty smee
I've brewed the perfect cup of tea.

Christine Bentley
Britain

Witches' Menu

Live lizard, dead lizard
Marinated, fried.
Poached lizard, pickled lizard
Salty lizard hide.

Hot lizard, cold lizard
Lizard over ice.
Baked lizard, boiled lizard
Lizard served with spice.

Sweet lizard, sour lizard
Smoked lizard heart.
Leg of lizard, loin of lizard
Lizard à la carte.

Sonja Nikolay
United States

Spell to Find a Lost Season Ticket

Stay, if fallen on the floor;
Flap, if hidden behind a door;
Jump, if in some guilty pocket;
Hear me, hear me,
Season ticket!
If I sing the spell in vain,
I cannot come to school again.

Ian Serraillier
Britain

Follow-on

Try to find more old spells and charms and make an illustrated collection. Make up your own recipe for a witch's brew, like Wes Magee, or devise a magic chant, like Christine Bentley.

The four poems in this section are called alphabet poems. The poets have taken the alphabet to give a pattern or structure to their words.

In *A was an Archer* on page 68 the various occupations have been chosen, in *Alphabet of Love* on page 66 and *Our Alphabetical Class* below the poets select children's names, and contained in Pete Morgan's clever and original alphabet poem on page 67 is an unusual valentine.

Our Alphabetical Class

Alice is always awake and alert,
Ben's best friend is his burly mate Bert.
Charles is cheerfully chummy and charms
Doris whose daring drums up alarms.
Ethel is everything everyone envies,
Frank is famed for his frenetic frenzies.
Georgina is gorgeous, generous and grand,
Harry is hazardous and well out of hand.
Iris is impetuous and gets into scrapes,
Jim likes a joke and jolly good japes.
Ken is keen on karate and kites,
Lisa is lively and likes the night lights.
Michael is moody and mopes round the place,
Nina is naughty and really not 'nace'.
Oliver's old fashioned and does what he ought,
Peter is proud and wins prizes at sport.
Quentin is quarrelsome and often quite stressful,
Rosey is rotund, red cheeked and restful.
Sidney is strident and shouts at the sky,
Teresa is timid and terribly shy.
Ursula's uncle is right round the bend,
Victor's a very valuable friend.
Wally is watchful and knows all the ways,
Xania makes excellent exits in plays.
Yasmine is a youthful go-getting girl,
Zelda is zealous and sports a kiss curl.

John Cotton
Britain

Alphabet of Love

April loves
Barry but he adores
Cheryl who only likes
David with the dark brown eyes
Elsie ignores
Felicity who can't stand
Georgina who really hates
Harriet who is always telling lies!
Ian sits with
Jason and they talk about
Katy who stares through large blue spectacles at
Leonard who she hates!
Maureen shouts at
Noleen for telling all her secrets to
Olivia and
Prudence and all her other mates.
Quentin's pal is
Russell and they come to school together with
Simon and
Timothy and
Uriah on their bikes
Veronica comes in Daddy's Porsche and
Wendy with her grandma and
Xavier, he stays at home and does just as he likes.
Yvonne-Marie for all to see loves only little
Zebedee.

Christine Bentley
Britain

An Apple Peel Valentine

A can band her eyes with black
B can not divide
C can test the str ength of love
D can never hide

E has three within her head
F has faithful two
G has crossed her tongue with lies
H is always true

J can beckon all before her
K can point to love and hate
L can set her right again
M can only stand and wait

N goes up and won't come down
O is blind to such good grace
P is always buxom P
Q will pull a yahoo face

R can walk in wanderlust
S can slip in slime
T can see no sight of stars
U might reach in time

V has stretched in supplication
W will win
Y has opened up her heart
and Z will sin, will sin

now X alone can come to trust
and love
without the quiz
that takes away the mystery
and tells her
who I is.

Pete Morgan
Britain

A was an Archer

A was an Archer
  who shot at a frog

B was a Butcher
  who kept a bull-dog

C was a Captain
  all covered with lace

D was a Drummer
  who played with much grace

E was an Esquire
  with pride on his brow

F was a Farmer
  who followed the plough

G was a Gamester
  who had but ill-luck

H was a Hunter
  and hunted a buck

I was an Italian
  who had a white mouse

J was a Joiner
  and built up a house

K was a King
  so mighty and grand

L was a Lady
  who had a white hand

M was a Miser
  who hoarded up gold

N was a Nobleman
    gallant and bold

O was an Organ boy
    who played about town

P was a Parson
    who wore a black gown

Q was a Queen
    who was fond of her people

R was a Robin
    who perched on a steeple

S was a Sailor
    who spent all he got

T was a Tinker
    who mended a pot

U was an Usher
    who taught little boys

V was a Veteran
    who sold pretty toys

W was a Watchman
    who guarded the door

X was eXpensive
    and so became poor

Y was a Youth
who did not love school

Z was a Zany
who looked a great fool.

Anonymous

Follow-on

Make up your own alphabet poem. It does not have to rhyme and you might have to leave out a few difficult letters such as X.

- Decide on a subject. It could be:

animals, monsters, birds or names - of people, street names, places, occupations.

- Write the alphabet down the left hand side of a piece of paper.
- Fill in the names of people or animals or whatever you choose. You may need a dictionary, telephone directory, specialist reference books to help you.

To get the idea you might begin by making a list of imaginary football teams or pop groups, choosing names which are as absurd and unusual as possible. Here are the beginnings of two written by Philip Johnson, age 12:

Pop Groups	Football Teams
Angry Angels	Arfhearted Dribblers
Batswhiskers	Brickboots United
Culture Vultures	Clodhoppers Eleven
Demonbusters	Donothing Rovers
Electric Plums	Endofseason Wanderers
Freddie and the Feetwobblers	Footinmouth Rangers

A more difficult alphabet poem is one where you choose words and phrases to follow each of the twenty-six letters to conjure up pictures in the reader's mind. Here is the beginning of one written by Shirley Stringer, age 13:

A is for alligator, snip-snap jawed
B is for bull, black bellowing brute
C is for cat, soft cushion of fur
D is for donkey, dusty grey and stubborn
E is for elephant, jungle's moving mountain
F is for fox, sly-forest, red fur.

- When you write out your alphabet poem, make the first letter of each line big and colourful so it stands out.
- You might try a class alphabet poem. To do this you need to write the alphabet on a large piece of paper and pin it to the wall. You and your friends can then take it in turns to complete a line.

Acrostics

Acrostics are poems where the first letter of each line forms the word.

December

W ater
I ces
N aked
T rees;
E arth
R ests.

Judith Nicholls
Britain

Crab

Crafty hunter
Racing slantways
Across the shore:
Baleful bone-box.

John Cunliffe
Britain

My Glasses

M - Meaningful

Y - Yes my glasses are meaningful

G - Grip my head at the sides

L - Love is strong so are my glasses

A - Attached to my head at the sides

S - Stop me walking into opticians

S - See through

E - Ever so clean

S - Seven quid

John Hegley
Britain

Dad

Dozing in his easy chair,
Asleep and snoring,
Deep in dreams of when he was young.

Dandruff on his collar
And an ever-growing paunch,
Drab old jumper and baggy pants.

Does he remember when I was little
And held his hand in the sand in the sun?
Does he know how I love him?

DAD of mine.

Collette Chapple, age 12

First Born

Hear her first sharp cry
And see her:
Pink and panting,
Pouting little lips,
In mother's arms.
New arrival, tiny miracle,
Elf-like,
Soft little bundle -
She.

Lesley Chapman, age 14

Skinhead

Big-booted brute,
Ugly face leering and sneering,
Little pig eyes, shiny as beads,
Long eagle nose, sharp as a hook.
You have more hair than brains!

Jonathan James, age 14

Yeti

You
Enormous
Tibetan
Iceman

Gervase Phinn
Britain

Dreams

Dirty little child with sticky nose,
Red-rimmed eyes and sparrow legs,
Empty belly and hand-me-down clothes,
And nothing his, save what he begs.
Maybe the Christian in us should see:
'Suffer little children to come to me.'

Jane Peace, age 14

Follow-on

• Write your own acrostic and try to capture in your poem the essential features of your subject.

You might pick:

a name - your own, a friend, brother or sister, uncle or aunt

an animal - lion, mouse, prehistoric

an insect - caterpillar, butterfly

a mood or feeling - rage, terror, loneliness, hatred, love

a place - your school, town, country.

R i d d l e s

Words can be tricky and troublesome things at times - particularly when poets use them to write riddles. Riddles are word puzzles, very cleverly written and fun to work out.

The riddles in the selection are only a few of the many thousands which exist, and they are all different. Some are of one line, others long and detailed; some are easy to solve, others very difficult; some are nine hundred years old, others very modern; some rhyme, others don't; and they come from many parts of the world, written in many different languages. Your will find the answers on page 80.

A white bird floats down through the air
And never a tree but he lights there.

Anonymous
Britain

I like to sit,
In a warm place;
I breathe water,
And sing with it,
Then scream
Until
You pull my nose off.

John Cunliffe
Britain

Who, sir, am I?
For a start, I hate sunshine
And deserve the penalty -
To be swallowed with good
    wine.
Miserable slitherer,
Landlubberly crustacean;
The French eat me, sir.
They are a wise nation!

John Mole
Britain

Riddles

A swan flew over the shifting field,
and came flying home without wings.

Traditional
Yugoslavia
Translated by A. Pennington

A city of thousands,
Yet no word is spoken.
There are great stores of gold,
But no money.
Some live imprisoned in cells,
Yet are good citizens.
Their six-legged cows
Give sweet milk;
They have no king -
But a queen rules and serves them.

John Cunliffe
Britain

A house full, a hole full,
And you cannot gather a bowl full.

Anonymous
Britain

76

Here's a thing:
Sixteen working,
Sixteen resting,
Two shepherds,
Two listeners,
And one a-stare.

Traditional
Malta
Translated by A. Arberry

In former days my mother and father
Forsook me for dead, for the fullness of life
Was not yet within me. But another woman
Graciously fitted me out in soft garments,
As kind to me as to her own children,
Tended and took me under her wing:
Until under her shelter, unlike her kin,
I matured as a mighty bird (as was my fate).
My guardian then fed me until I could fly,
And could wander more widely on my
Excursions; she had the less of her own
Sons and daughters by what she did thus.

Traditional Old English
Translated by K. Crossley-Holland

I am the shame beneath a carpet.
No one comes to sweep me off my feet.

Abandoned rooms and unread books collect me.
Sometimes I dance like particles of light.

My legions thicken on each window pane,
A gathering of dusk, perpetual gloom.

And when at last the house has fallen,
I am the cloud left hanging in the air.

John Mole
Britain

Allow me to describe myself.
I live upon a dusty shelf,
With other sorts who do the same.
I have a title to my name,
Yet wear a jacket without sleeves.
I'm not a plant, but I have leaves.
(It's also true I'm not a tree,
Though that is what I *used* to be.)
I'm full of words, but cannot speak,
I sometimes vanish for a week,
and then return to my dear nook.
You've guessed it - I'm a library book!

Colin West
Britain

This creature has ten tongues, twenty eyes, forty feet
and walks with difficulty.

Traditional Viking
Scandinavia
Translated by K. Crossley-Holland

Four Yoruba riddles

Two tiny birds jump over two hundred trees.

The black one is squatting - the red one is licking his bottom.

A round calabash in the spear grass.

A thin staff reaches from heaven to earth.

Traditional Yoruba
Nigeria
Translated by U. Beier

This wind wafts little creatures
High over the hill-slopes. They are very
Swarthy, clad in coats of black.
They travel here and there all together,
Singing loudly, liberal with their songs.
Their haunts are wooded cliffs, yet they sometimes
Come to the houses of men. Name them yourselves.

Traditional Old English
Translated by K. Crossley-Holland

Follow-on

With a partner, read some of the riddles where no answer is given. Try to solve these word puzzles before checking the answers below. Now, still with a partner, make up some riddles of your own, the more ingenious the better.

- Decide on a subject. It could be:

  an object - knife, hammer, telephone
  an animal - horse, pig, crocodile
  elements - wind, fire, water
  a vegetable - onion, cabbage, carrot
  a flower - rose, tulip, dandelion clock
  transport - train, bus, bicycle.

- Discuss and jot down the ideas that come into your head when you think about your chosen subject.

- Try to create a word picture or image of your subject in your mind. Like the writers of the riddles in this selection, try to use some metaphors and similes to make your words vivid and unusual.

- Decide whether your riddle is a one-liner or a longer, more detailed puzzle. Will it rhyme or not?

- Try your riddle out on others in your class.

- Collect all the riddles together in a class 'Riddle-Me-Ree' anthology, or mount them on a wall display with picture clues.

Answers to riddles

'A white bird floats ...' - snow
'I like to sit ...' - a kettle
'Who, sir, am I?' - a snail
'A swan flew over ...' - a sailing ship
'A city of thousands' - a beehive
'A house full, a hole full' - fog
'Here's a thing' - a face
'In former days ...' - a cuckoo
'I am the shame beneath the carpet' - dust

'This creature has ten tongues ...' - a sow with nine piglets
'Two tiny birds ...' - eyes
'The black one ...' - a cooking pot on the fire
'A round calabash ...' - the moon and stars
'A thin staff ...' - rain
'This wind wafts little creatures ...' - house martins

The way the words of a poem are arranged on the page is important. In William Hart-Smith's poem the words appear long and narrow like the shape of the razor fish. The shape of Christine Bentley's poem, a rain shower of words, adds to the feeling of loneliness and longing and in Roger McGough's *Watchwords* the words appear to have lives of their own as they scurry across the page. In *Invasion* the words increase in size to give the impression of the gulls slowly getting nearer and nearer, and in Max Fatchen's poem the words trace the outline of a page of writing.

These shape poems are sometimes called calligrams and are fun to create.

O my!

He rocked the boat,
Did Ezra Shank;
These bubbles mark

o

o

o

o

o

o

o

o

o

o

o

o

o

Where Ezra sank.

Anonymous

Balloon

a s

big as

ball as round

as sun ... I tug

and pull you when

you run and when

wind blows I

say polite

ly

H

O

L

D

M

E

T

I

G

H

T

L

Y.

Colleen Thibaudeau

Razor Fish

If you were
to draw
lightly
a straight line
right
down
the margin
of this
sheet of
paper
with your
pen
it wouldn't be
as thin
as a
Razor Fish
seen
edge
ways
on

If you were
to cut
the shape
of a
fish
out of transparent
cellophane
with a
tiny
tail fin
and a mouth
as long
and sharp
as
a
pin
and let it drift
tail up
head down
you wouldn't see -

the Razor Fish
See
what
I
mean?

William Hart-Smith
New Zealand

Exactly like a 'V'

When my brother Tommy
Sleeps in bed with me
He doubles up
And makes
himself
exactly
like
a
V

And 'cause the bed is not so wide
A part of him is on my side.

Abram Bunn Ross
United States

Watchwords

watch the words
watch words the
watchword is
watch words are
sly as boots
ifyoutakeyoureyesoffthemforaminute

up

and   they're   and

away

allover

the

place

Roger McGough
Britain

Downpour

It's raining, raining, pouring, raining, gushing, raining, slicing down,
Filling guttering, gushing, spluttering, forming puddles through the town.
It's making all the rooftops oily, black and shiny, wet and stark.
Running rivers down the windows, dreary and dismal, cold and dark.
It's raining, raining, pouring, raining, gushing, raining, slicing down,
Weeping, seeping, pounding, leaping, splattering, spitting – I might drown!

Christine Bentley
Britain

83

Invasion

WITH THE FIRST
THE GULLS   EDGE OF LIGHT
          CAME BEATING IN
          FROM THE SEA
          OVER

THE FARMLAND INTO
          ROOFCOUNTRY, DUST-
BIN COUNTRY, WAKING THE
          TOWN

FROM ITS SUNDAY
          MORNING BED. THEY
          FILLED THE AIR WITH THE
          SCREAMS

          FILLED THE PALE
OF THEIR DISSENSION,
          SKY WITH THEIR   ARROGANT
          STRONG

          WEAVING THEY BUILT
WINGS. WHEELING AND
A TOWERING PATTERN OF FLIGHT
          ABOVE THE
          TOWN.

Pamela Gillilan
Britain

84

Holiday Memories

IT WAS  COLD

AND I WAS FEELING REALLY

AND 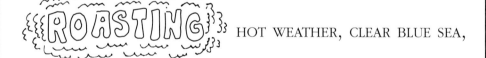 TO THE SKIN!

I REMEMBERED THE FANTASTIC HOLIDAY IN SPAIN -

 HOT WEATHER, CLEAR BLUE SEA,

BEACHES AND A CLEAR CLEAR SKY.

NOW IT'S ALL A MEMORY.

Paula Edwards, age 14

85

Wall walk

THIN
WALL.
STEEP   FALL.
STEP
CARE-
FULLY
ARMS   OUT.
TIP   TIP
BUT
NOT
TOO
MUCH
TIP.
BAL-
ANCE.
AH.
MADE IT.

Robert Froman
Britain

Heart

```
        F
    N  L        Y
 W      A     M  H
 O      M  M     E
 D        E      A
 D               R
    I          T
     S       L
      P     I
       U   K
        N E
         A
```

Mirror

```
           IN
      IONS      THIS
      FLECT      MIR
       RE        ROR
       THE        I
       LIKE       AM
       NOT        EN
      AND       CLOSED
       GELS       A
        AN       LIVE
       GINE      AND
        MA       REAL
         I   AS
          YOU
```

Guillaume Apollinaire
France
Translated by O. Bernard

I
NEED
CONTACT
L E N S E S

like I need a poke in the eye

John Hegley
Britain

The Allivator

at the top.
                then eat you
            his back
          ride upon
        let you
      he will
    in a shop
  see one
if you
allivator
Beware the

Roger McGough
Britain

Follow-on

Make up a shape poem, turning your words into the picture of your chosen subject.

- Decide on a subject. It could be:
  a part of your body - eyes, feet, nose
  a fruit - pineapple, banana, pear
  an animal - cat, elephant, giraffe
  a fish - shark, eel, jellyfish
  a shape - heart, star, diamond, crown.

- Jot down all the words that come into your head when you think about this subject.

- Draw a simple outline shape and arrange the words to fit into it.

- Cut out your shape and mount it in a class anthology or on a wall display.

Poets not only describe what they see and hear around them, their feelings and thoughts, wishes and sensations, they also use poetry to tell stories or 'narratives' - they write narrative verse.

The first four poems in this section are cautionary tales, amusing and clever and containing a warning or moral. They have a regular rhyme scheme of AABBCC and a regular rhythm of four beats or stresses to each line.

Lord Ullin's Daughter is a very different kind of story poem. It is a ballad. The earliest narrative poems in English are the ballads, anonymously written and passed from generation to generation by word of mouth. *Lord Ullin's Daughter* is typical of a ballad poem. It has a regular rhyme scheme of ABAB and a regular rhythm of 4:3:4:3 beats to a verse of four lines. Like the ballads written four hundred years ago, this poem has the same pounding rhythms, fast action and tragic end.

Henry King

Who chewed bits of String, and was early cut off in
Dreadful Agonies

The Chief Defect of Henry King
Was chewing little bits of String.
At last he swallowed some which tied
Itself in ugly Knots inside.
Physicians of the Utmost Fame
Were called at once; but when they came
They answered, as they took their Fees,
There is no Cure for this Disease.
Henry will very soon be dead.
His Parents stood about his Bed
Lamenting his Untimely Death,
When Henry, with his Latest Breath,
Cried - 'Oh, my Friends, be warned by me,
That Breakfast, Dinner, Lunch, and Tea
Are all the Human Frame requires ...'
With that, the Wretched Child expires.

Hilaire Belloc
Britain

Kenneth

Who was too fond of bubble-gum and met an untimely end

The chief defect of Kenneth Plumb
Was chewing too much bubble-gum.
He chewed away with all his might,
Morning, evening, noon and night.
Even (oh, it makes you weep)
Blowing bubbles in his sleep.

He simply couldn't get enough!
His face was covered with the stuff.
As for his teeth - oh, what a sight!
It was a wonder he could bite.
His loving mother and his dad
Both remonstrated with the lad.

Ken repaid them for the trouble
By blowing yet another bubble.

'Twas no joke. It isn't funny
Spending all your pocket money
On the day's supply of gum -
Sometimes Kenny felt quite glum.
As he grew, so did his need -
There seemed no limit to his greed:
At ten he often put away
Ninety-seven packs a day.

Then at last he went too far -
Sitting in his father's car,
Stuffing gum without a pause,
Found that he had jammed his jaws.
He nudged his dad and pointed to
The mouthful that he couldn't chew.
'Well, spit it out if you can't chew it!'
Ken shook his head. He couldn't do it.

Before long he began to groan -
The gum was solid as a stone
Dad took him to a builder's yard;
They couldn't help. It was too hard.

They called a doctor and he said,
'This silly boy will soon be dead.
His mouth's so full of bubble-gum
No nourishment can reach his tum.'

Remember Ken and please do not
Go buying too much you-know-what.

Wendy Cope
Britain

On Monday Morning

There's been a break-in
down at the school
and our classroom's been wrecked
by some stupid fool.

The police have arrived
all smart-dressed and slim.
Our teachers are cross.
The Head's looking grim.

Six windows are broken.
We must wait in the Hall
but there's nothing to do
so we stare at the wall.

They've paint-sprayed the desks,
thrown books on the floor,
snapped off all our plants
and kicked in the door.

That room was our home,
we worked there with pride
but now it's a wreck
and we can't go inside.

Detectives are searching
for footprints and clues.
We're still in our coats
and full of the blues.

One boy's heard a rumour,
he gives name and address.
Now the caretaker's here
to clear up the mess.

Much later that morning
we're back in our place.
Card over the windows.
It's all a disgrace.

The vandals stole pens.
Our hamster's not fed.
There's pain in my heart,
an ache in my head.

There's been a break-in
down at the school
and our classroom's been wrecked
by some stupid fool.

Wes Magee
Britain

92

The Ballad of Johnny Shiner

A story for harvest festival

This is the tale
Of Johnny Shiner,
Born in the year
Of forty-nine;
With brothers and sisters,
Three, four, five,
It was good to be alive;
In the sun and wind
To run.
Life a game
And full of fun.

Johnny grew up
And went to school,
And soon his head
Was teeming full,
Of sums and art
And other goodies,
And environmental
Studies!
'Whatever's that?'
Said Mum and Dad;
'It's about our world,'
Said the promising lad.
'The things we need
To live and grow,
Earth's good store
From the crops we sow,
The harvest of
The sea and land,
Blessed by the
Almighty's hand.'

Johnny did well,
He did not shirk,
School was finished,
Time for work.
Out into
The world of men,
Stepped our clever
Johnny then.
'What shall I do,
With my arm so strong,
To help the folks
I live among?
Where is the work,
Fit to my hand,
To make life good
In our fair land?'

Johnny Shiner,
Johnny Shiner,
You shall go
To be a miner.

Johnny joined
His fellow men,
Stepped in the cage,
And the gate clashed, then,
Down he dropped
Into the earth,
And Johnny he prayed
For all his worth;
'Please God bring me
Safe again,
Into the sun
And wind
And rain.'

Johnny picked up
His pick and lamp,
Crouched down low
In the dark and damp.
Hacked at the coal
In a three-foot seam,
Thought school and childhood
Just a dream.

Seven long years
Our Johnny worked,
Never faltered
Never shirked.
Then came the word
On the news at nine,
FIFTY MINERS
TRAPPED DOWN THE MINE.
Johnny, wakened
From a dream,
Rushed to join
The rescue team.
They dug out forty
Safe and sound,
But ten were lost
Deep underground.

And later,
When the names were read,
Johnny knew his
Friend was dead.

So Johnny he up
And walked away,
To live and fight
Another day.
'I'll work,' said he,
'In the sun and the rain,
My harvest to be
The golden grain.'
Then Johnny Shiner
Prayed to the Lord,
'Oh let your people
Hear the word,
The sun and the rain
Are all we need,
With the fertile earth
And the growing seed,
The wind and the river,
That flows from the hills,
Can give us power
And turn our mills.
The harvest of lives
In the murderous mine,
Can be no part
Of a plan of thine.
Let us harvest the earth
Yet keep it whole,
For earth is precious,
Earth is small.'

And Johnny Shiner
Said Amen.
And Johnny Shiner
Said Amen.

John Cunliffe
Britain

Lord Ullin's Daughter

A chieftain, to the Highlands bound,
Cries, 'Boatman, do not tarry!
And I'll give thee a silver pound
To row us o'er the ferry.'

'Now who be ye, would cross
    Lochgyle,
This dark and stormy water?'
'Oh, I'm the chief of Ulva's isle,
And this Lord Ullin's daughter.

'And fast before her father's men
Three days we've fled together;
For should he find us in the glen,
My blood would stain the heather.

'His horsemen hard behind us ride;
Should they our steps discover,
Then who will cheer my bonny bride
When they have slain her lover?'

Out spoke the hardy Highland wight,
'I'll go, my chief - I'm ready.
It is not for your silver bright,
But for your winsome lady.

'And by my word! the bonny bird
In danger shall not tarry;
So though the waves are raging white,
I'll row you o'er the ferry.'

By this the storm grew loud apace;
The water-wraith was shrieking;
And in the scowl of heaven each face
Grew dark as they were speaking.

But still as wilder blew the wind,
And as the night grew dearer,
Adown the glen rode armed men -
Their trampling sounded nearer.

'O haste thee, haste!' the lady cries,
'Though tempests round us gather;
I'll meet the raging of the skies,
But not an angry father.'

The boat has left a stormy land,
A stormy sea before her -
When, O! too strong for human hand,
The tempest gathered o'er her.

And still they rowed amidst the roar
Of waters fast prevailing -
Lord Ullin reached that fatal shore;
His wrath was changed to wailing.

For sore dismayed through storm and
    shade
His child he did discover;
One lovely hand she stretched for aid,
And one was round her lover.

'Come back! come back!' he cried in
    grief,
'Across this stormy water;
And I'll forgive your Highland chief,
My daughter! - O my daughter!'

'Twas vain - the loud waves lashed
    the shore,
Return or aid preventing.
The waters wild went o'er his child,
And he was left lamenting.

Thomas Campbell
Britain

95

Follow-on

On Monday Morning and *The Ballad of Johnny Shiner* are powerful modern narrative poems. In what ways are they different from *Lord Ullin's Daughter*?

You might think about:
- the subject
- rhyme scheme
- rhythm - beats to each line
- number of verses
- verse length
- the words used.

• Try writing a cautionary tale of your own. Remember the rhyme scheme needs to be AABBCC and the rhythm regular with four beats to each line. You might like to continue one of the following:

1 What a liar was little Ruth!
She never ever told the truth ...

2 Noleen was a naughty child
Who drove her mum and dad quite wild ...

3 When all his brothers were asleep,
Down the stairs young Tim would creep ...

4 A cheeky child was Ermintrude,
Who everyone thought very rude ...

You might want to choose your own subject. It could be a boy who slammed doors or was cruel to animals, or a girl who ate too much or had a fearful temper.

• Try writing a ballad. You might tell a story you have heard on the television or read in the newspaper, or you might recount an incident which happened at school. Remember to keep your verses to four lines and make your rhythms and rhymes regular.

• Write out one of the cautionary tales or ballads as a story or a play.

• Act out in small groups the story of *Lord Ullin's Daughter*. Imagine what happened before the poem began.

• Prepare a reading of one of these poems in this section and 'perform' it. You might present the poem with a partner or as a group.

In this section is a variety of poems: telephone poems, letter poems, 'Teacher, Teacher' poems and conversation poems - and all cry out for reading aloud.

Daley's Dorg, Wattle

'You can talk about yer sheep dorgs,' said the man from Allan's Creek,
'But I know a dorg that simply knocked 'em bandy!
Do whatever you would show him, and you'd hardly need to speak.
Owned by Daley, drover cove in Jackandandy.

'We was talkin' in the parlour, me and Daley, quiet like,
When a blowfly starts a-buzzin' round the ceilin',
Up gets Daley, and he says to me, "You wait a minute, Mike.
And I'll show you what a dorg he is at heelin'."

'And an empty pickle-bottle was a-standin' on the shelf,
Daley takes it down and puts it on the table,
And he bets me drinks that blinded dorg would do it by himself-
And I didn't think as how as he was able!

'Well, he shows the dorg the bottle, and he points up to the fly,
And he shuts the door, and says to him - "Now Wattle!"
And in less than fifteen seconds, spare me days, it ain't a lie,
That there dorg had got that inseck in the bottle!'

W.T. Goodge
Britain

97

Conversation Piece

Late again Blenkinsop?
What's the excuse this time?
Not my fault sir.
Whose fault is it then?
Grandma's sir.
Grandma's. What did she do?
She died sir.
Died?
She's seriously dead all right sir.
That makes four grandmothers this term.
And all on P.E. days Blenkinsop.
I know. It's very upsetting sir.
How many grandmothers have you got Blenkinsop?
Grandmothers sir? None sir.
None?
All dead sir.
And what about yesterday Blenkinsop?
What about yesterday sir?
You missed maths.
That was the dentist sir.
The dentist died?
No sir. My teeth sir.
You missed the test Blenkinsop.
I'd been looking forward to it too sir.
Right, line up for P.E.
Can't sir.
No such word as can't. Why can't you?
No kit sir.
Where is it?
Home sir.
What's it doing at home?
Not ironed sir.
Couldn't you iron it?
Can't do it sir.
Why not?
My hand sir.
Who usually does it?
Grandma sir.
Why couldn't she do it?
Dead sir.

Gareth Owen
Britain

98

Joke

Mother shouts in dead of night
'You're crying son, are you all right?'
Says Son with sobs from room next door:
'It's school, I won't go there no more.'
Says Mum 'You have to, please don't cry.'
'I won't and I've three reasons why,
the teachers loathe me, hate my guts
the kids attack me, think I'm nuts,
they abuse me when I do my work,
One day Mum, I'll go berserk!'
Says Mum 'Although these things I know,
I've one good reason you must go
Although these things fill you with dread
You're 46 and you're the Head!'

Alan Gilbey
Britain

An Urgent Call to the Dentist

Dentist! Dentist!
I've got toothache!
It's like the bite of a poison-
    snake!
Dentist! Dentist!
Do something quick!
I'm very very very sick.
Dentist! Dentist!
Pull it out!
I promise, honest,
I will not shout!
I don't even care,
If I have to pay,
I'll get on the bike,
And come right away.

Ouch! Stoppit!
Blood and thunder!
Dentist! Dentist!
You've made a blunder!
And just look how
My blood keeps spurting!
And I do believe,
My tooth's still hurting!
Dentist! Dentist!
I tell the truth!
You've gone and pulled ...
You've pulled the wrong tooth!

John Cunliffe
Britain

Christmas Thank-yous

Dear Auntie

Oh what a nice jumper
I've always adored powder blue
and fancy you thinking of
orange and pink
for the stripes
how clever of you!

Dear Cousin

What socks!
And the same sort you wear,
so you must be
the last word in style
and I'm certain you're right that the
luminous green
will make me stand out a mile.

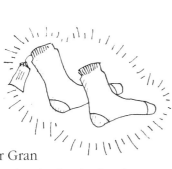

Dear Gran

Many thanks for the hankies
Now I really can't wait for the 'flu
and the daisies embroidered
in red round the 'M'
for Michael
how
thoughtful of you!

Dear Uncle

The soap is
terrific
So
useful
and such a kind thought and
how did you guess that
I'd just used the last of
the soap the last Christmas brought?

Dear Sister

I quite understand your concern
It's a risk sending jam in the post
But I think I've pulled out
all the big bits
of glass
so it won't taste too sharp
spread on toast.

Dear Grandad

Don't fret
I'm delighted
So don't think your gift will
offend
I'm not at all hurt
that you gave up this year
and just sent me
a fiver
to spend

Mick Gowar
Britain

Growing

When I grow up I'll be so kind,
Not yelling 'Now' or 'Do you MIND!'
Or making what is called a scene,
Like 'So you're back' or 'Where've you BEEN.'
Or 'Goodness, child, what is it NOW?'
Or saying 'STOP ... that awful row',
Or 'There's a time and place to eat'
And 'Wipe your nose' or 'Wipe your feet'.
I'll just let people go their way
And have an extra hour for play.
No angry shouting 'NOW what's wrong?'
It's just that growing takes so long.

Max Fatchen

Mum, can I go Out?

Me   Mum, can I go out?
Mum Out where?
Me   In the village, where else?
Mum Where in the village?
Me   I dunno - around.
Mum Whereabouts?
Me   Just around.
Mum Who's going to be out?
Me   Just the gang.
Mum Who's going to be out?
Me   Just the gang.
Mum Who's the gang?
Me   The gang's the gang, Mum.
Mum What time will you be coming in?
Me   About 9.30.
Mum Isn't it dark then?
Me   Yer, why?
Mum But young girls shouldn't ...
Me   OK Mum, you always say that. Well can I go out?
Mum NO!!!

Helen Cranswick
Britain

Get Off this Estate

'Get off this estate.'
'What for?'
'Because it's mine.'
'Where did you get it?'
'From my father.'
'Where did he get it?'
'From his father.'
'And where did he get it?'
'He fought for it.'
'Well, I'll fight you for it.'

Carl Sandburg
United States

Storytime

Once upon a time, children,
there lived a fearsome dragon ...

Please, miss,
Jamie's made a dragon.
Out in the sandpit.

Lovely, Andrew.
Now this dragon
had enormous red eyes
and a swirling, whirling tail ...

Jamie's dragon's got
yellow eyes, miss.

Lovely, Andrew.
Now this dragon was
as wide as a horse
as green as the grass
as tall as a house ...

Jamie's would JUST fit
in our classroom, miss!

But he was a very friendly
     dragon ...

Jamie's dragon ISN'T, miss.
He eats people, miss.
Especially TEACHERS,
Jamie said.

Very nice, Andrew!
Now one day, children,
this enormous dragon
rolled his red eye,
whirled his swirly green tail
and set off to find ...

His dinner, miss!
Because he was hungry, miss!

Thank you, Andrew.
He rolled his red eye,
whirled his green tail,
and opened his wide, wide
     mouth
until

Please, miss,
I did try to tell you, miss!

Judith Nicholls
Britain

Mars To Earth

MARS, THE GOD OF WAR
TO EARTH, MEN OF PEACE.

MARS   HELLO, THIS IS MARS. CAN YOU HEAR ME, EARTH?
EARTH   yes, we can hear you. Speak to us.
MARS   I WISH TO SPEAK TO THE MEN OF PEACE.
EARTH   we are those people. Speak in truth.
MARS   NO. NOT TO THE LEADERS OF THE WORLD.
EARTH   but we are the GREATEST OF ALL MANKIND.
MARS   NO. I WOULD SPEAK TO THE meekest minds.
EARTH   THEY'RE NOT IMPORTANT. YOU WOULDN'T BE HEARD.
MARS   I will not talk to the ones who shout.
EARTH   BUT WE ARE THE ONES WHO WIN ALL WARS.
MARS   You are the ones who'll destroy the stars.
EARTH   WHAT ON EARTH IS THIS TALK ABOUT?
MARS   War and peace. I will speak no more.
EARTH   SPEAK UP, MARS. YOUR SIGNAL'S LOST.
           WE'VE LOST ALL CONTACT. MARS IS A GHOST.

    we're the children of earth, mars. whisper. we hear.

Berlie Doherty
Britain

Awo! (Thank you!)

Women who never have to hoe, awo!
Give me a hoe that doesn't dig, awo!
They have tied a handle to the blade, awo!
Tied it tightly just the wr ong way, awo!
Let me clear the field, awo!
Dig, let me dig, let me dig! A wo!
And I will have fat meat, awo!
Now just let me weed, awo!
Let me try to walk, awo!
My back is killing me, awo!

Anonymous
Uganda

Guinea corn

Guinea corn, I long to see you
Guinea corn, I long to plant you
Guinea corn, I long to mould you
Guinea corn, I long to weed you
Guinea corn, I long to hoe you
Guinea corn, I long to top you
Guinea corn, I long to cut you
Guinea corn, I long to dry you
Guinea corn, I long to beat you
Guinea corn, I long to trash you
Guinea corn, I long to parch you
Guinea corn, I long to grind you
Guinea corn, I long to turn you
Guinea corn, I long to eat you

Anonymous
Jamaica

If You Want To See An Alligator

If you want to see an alligator
you must go down to the muddy slushy
end of the old Caroony River

I know an alligator
who's living down there -
She's a-Mean. She's a-Big. She's a-Wicked
She's a-Fierce.

Yes, if you really want to see
an alligator, you must go down to the
muddy slushy end of the old Caroony River

Go down gently to that River and say,
'Alligator Mama
Alligator Mama
Alligator Mamaaaaaaaaaaa'

And up she'll rise
But don't stick around
RUN FOR YOUR LIFE!

Grace Nichols
Guyana/Britain

Follow-on

• In pairs or small groups, select a poem and prepare it for performance in front of the class. If you choose *Joke* or *Growing* one of you could read the dialogue (the actual words spoken) and the other the parts in between. In Berlie Doherty's poem and *Get Off this Estate*, each person could read an alternate line.

In *Christmas Thank-yous* each person in your group could read a verse and *Daley's Dorg, Wattle* could be presented chorally (where all the group perform the four verses).

• Try writing your own poem. It could be in the form of a letter: to an auntie, the Gas Board, a supermarket manager, a neighbour.

It could be a telephone poem: to the doctor, the vet, your teacher, a friend.

You might try a conversation poem between:

- you and your brother or sister
- you and your teacher
- your mum or dad and a neighbour
- two angry motorists
- a policeman and a burglar
- a king and a beggar

or any two people who have differing views.

Epitaphs

Epitaphs are words carved on tombstones. Usually they are simple and sad, and they can often be very moving, like these two seen in a Doncaster graveyard:

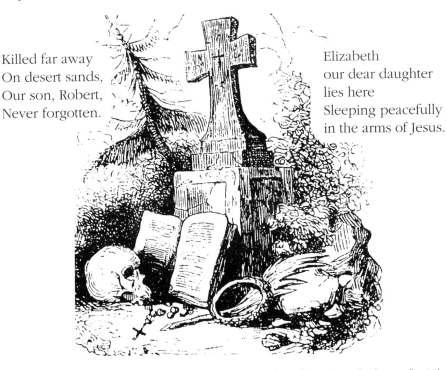

Killed far away
On desert sands,
Our son, Robert,
Never forgotten.

Elizabeth
our dear daughter
lies here
Sleeping peacefully
in the arms of Jesus.

Sometimes epitaphs can be clever and very amusing. Occasionally they reflect the occupations of those buried beneath, like many of those in this selection.

A schoolmistress called Binks lies here.
She held her own for twenty year.
She pleaded, biffed, said: 'I'm your friend.'
But children got her in the end.

Here lies a greedy girl, Jane Bevan,
Whose breakfasts hardly ever stopped.
One morning at half past eleven
She snapped and crackled and then popped.

Roy Fuller
Britain

Eight Epitaphs

An admiral of the fleet lies here,
Who sailed the sea for forty year,
Over the bridge the tar did bend,
And sadly met a watery end.

The cobbler buried here is Bloggs,
Who breathed his last and popped his clogs.

In parachute Commando Stead,
Fell from a plane and dropped down dead.

This electrician's name was Smout,
He touched the wrong wire and his lights went out.

Here lieth window-cleaner Ducket,
Who fell from his ladder and kicked the bucket.

The candle-maker Thomas Muffit,
Reached one hundred and then did snuff it.

Here lies the vicar who felt so tired,
That after expounding, then expired.

A teacher Miss Pricilla Pye,
Now teaches angels on the sky.

Christine Bentley
Britain

On a Bus Conductor

Here lies the conductor
Of a forty-one bus;
At last he's reached
His terminus.

On a Weaver

She was not deft,
With her weft,
Now she winds her warp,
To the sound of a harp.

John Cunliffe
Britain

'Biby's' Epitaph

A muvver was barfin' 'er biby one night,
The youngest of ten and a tiny young mite,
The muvver was poor and the biby was thin,
Only a skelington covered in skin;
The muvver turned rahnd for the soap off the rack,
She was but a moment, but when she turned back,
The biby was gorn; and in anguish she cried,
'Oh, where is my biby?' - The angels replied:

'Your biby 'as fell dahn the plug 'ole,
Your biby 'as gorn dahn the plug;
The poor little thing was so skinny and thin
'E oughter been barfed in a jug;
Your biby is perfeckly 'appy,
'E won't need a barf any more,
Your biby 'as fell dahn the plug 'ole,
Not lorst, but gorn before.'

Anonymous
Britain

On Leslie Moore
Here lies what's left
of Leslie Moore.
No Les
No more.

Anonymous

Ici Au Printemps
*Found in Eckington
Hall, Nottinghamshire*
Ici au printemps de leur
jeunesse mes bien aimées
soeurs Louisa et Eliza
cultivaient des fleurs.
Hélas, elles ont passé
comme ces fleurs et
elles ont séché comme
l'herbe des champs.*

Anonymous

* *Translation: 'In the spring of their youth, my beloved sisters Louisa and Eliza used to grow flowers here. Alas, like those flowers they are no more, and like the meadow grass, they have withered.'*

Follow-on
Think up some amusing epitaphs. You might try to write some about people with the following occupations:

footballer	politician	teacher
bricklayer	police officer	doctor
husband	bus driver	jockey
wife	secretary	flight attendant

Spooky Poems, Sad Poems and Silly Poems

Anyone can write poetry and poems can be about anything: people and places, sounds and sights, objects and emotions.

Poems can be sad, funny, witty, violent, soft, vigorous, frightening, magical, macabre. Poems can be songs and speeches, rumours and riddles, moods and memories, lessons and lists. Poems can be whispered or chanted, shouted or sung, performed or recited.

In this section is a variety of poems. Some may make you chuckle, others may make you feel sad, some might make you think deeply or in a different way about something. Read these poems to yourself quietly - they might give you ideas for your own writing.

Spooky Poems

Asleep

A child said,
'There are people in our graveyard
who are not dead.
They are not dead at all,
but they are in graves.'

Ghosts?
Spooks?
Spectres?

I went to see for myself,
and there it was,
as plain as a pig!
The words were carved on the
      stone;
'In loving memory of Ethel,
Who fell asleep on the 13th May
      1910.'

I listened for sounds of snoring,
but all was silent.
Plainly, Ethel was a quiet sleeper,
but what an odd place for a sleep!
And surely it must be true?
Who would carve a lie so deeply in
      stone?
I listened again,
but all was silent.
What about the church-bells?
Wouldn't they waken her?
Then what?
Then what?

John Cunliffe
Britain

The Game ... at the Hallowe'en Party in Hangman's Wood

Around the trees ran witches
their nails as long as knives.
Behind a bush hid demons
in fear for their lives.

Murder, murder in the dark!
The screams ring in your ears.
It's just a game, a silly lark,
no need for floods of tears.

Tall ghosts and other nasties
jumped out and wailed like trains.
A skeleton in irons
kept rattling his chains.

Murder, murder in the dark!
The screams ring in your ears.
It's just a game, a silly lark,
so wipe away those tears.

A werewolf howled his heart out.
The Horrid Dwarf crept by.
There was blood upon his boots
and murder in his eye.

Murder, murder in the dark!
The screams ring in your ears.
It's just a game, a silly lark;
Oh, come now, no more tears.

Owls were hooting, 'Is it you?'
Until a wizard grim
pointed to the Dwarf and said,
'The murderer, it's him!'

Murder, murder in the dark!
The screams ring in your ears.
It's just a game, a silly lark;
there's no time left for tears.

Murder, murder in the dark!
The screams fade in the night.
Listen, there's a farm dog's bark!
And look, the dawn's first light!

Wes Magee
Britain

112

Phamily Phantoms

My father is a werewolf,
My mother is a witch,
My Auntie May's a vampire,
And lives inside a crypt.
My Uncle Stan's a goblin
And my Auntie Jean's a ghoul
And my cousin Tom's a little imp
And never goes to school.
My sister Pat's new husband
Is the Phantom of the Manor
He comes to life at midnight
And hits you with a spanner.
Our Maureen is a poltergeist
As so's my brother Bob
Who recently got married
To the Creature from the Bog.
My grandad is the Zombie
Who haunts the church at night
Dressed only in his underwear
He's not a pretty sight.
My grandma is an ancient spook
The daughter of a sprite
She roams around the neighbourhood
When you've turned out the light.
Uncle Paddy is a Leprechaun
Furry, fat and frisky
He lived in a distillery
And samples all the whisky.
Our Brenda is a banshee
And our Gary is a gremlin
And Philip is a fairy
But we don't talk about him.
It's strange that with these relatives
I'm as normal as can be
But it's magic when on Sunday
They all come round for tea.

Gervase Phinn
Britain

The Nokk

Be warned you little childr en
Every son and every daughter
Who disobey your mums and dads
And play too close to water.

For in every river, stream and brook,
In lake and pond and lock,
In waterfalls steep and chasms deep,
There lurks the deadly NOKK.

His beard is of a weedy green
His ears like giant oars,
His eyes are the hue of the ocean blue,
And his hands are giant claws.

He sits and waits in his watery cave,
And never makes a noise,
Or silently swims near the surface clear
Looking for girls and boys.

And should he spy a child like you,
Playing near waters deep,
With his click-clack jaws and his snip-snap claws
He'll grab you by the feet.

Then he'll drag you down to his murky depths,
To the watery world of the fish
And on his rock, the deadly NOKK
Will eat his tasty dish.

So be warned, you little children,
And obey your parents, do.
Every son, every daughter, stay away from the water,
Or his next meal might be you!

Gervase Phinn
Britain

The Stolen Child

Where dips the rocky highland
Of Sleuth Wood in the lake,
There lies a leafy island
Where flapping herons wake
The drowsy water rats;
There we've hid our faery vats,
Full of berries,
And of reddest stolen cherries.
Come away, O human child!
To the waters and the wild
With a faery, hand in hand,
For the world's more full of weeping than you can understand.

Where the wave of moonlight glosses
The dim grey sands with light
Far off by furthest Rosses
We foot it all the night,
Weaving olden dances,
Mingling hands and mingling glances
Till the moon has taken flight;
To and fro we leap
And chase the frothy bubbles,
While the world is full of troubles
And is anxious in its sleep.
Come away, O human child!
To the waters and the wild
With a faery, hand in hand,
For the world's more full of weeping than you can understand.

Where the wandering water gushes
From the hills above Glen-Car
In pools among the rushes
That scarce could bathe a star,
We seek for slumbering trout,
And whispering in their ears
Give them unquiet dreams;
Leaning softly out
From ferns that drop their tears
Over the young streams.
Come away, O human child!
To the waters and the wild
With a faery, hand in hand,
For the world's more full of weeping than you can understand

Away with us he's going,
The solemn-eyed:
He'll hear no more the lowing
Of the calves on the warm hillside
Or the kettle on the hob
Sing peace into his breast,
Or see the brown mice bob
Round and round the oatmeal chest.
For he comes, the human child,
To the waters, and the wild
With a faery, hand in hand,
From a world more full of weeping than he can understand.

W.B. Yeats
Ireland

Sad Poems

Mother to son

Well, son, I'll tell you:
Life for me ain't been no crystal stair .
It's had tacks in it,
And splinters,
And boards torn up,
And places with no carpet on the floor -
Bare.
But all the time
I'se been a-climbin' on,
And reachin' landin's,
And turnin' corners,
And sometimes goin' in the dark
Where there ain't been no light.
So boy, don't you tur n back.
Don't you set down on the steps
'Cause you finds it's kinder hard.
Don't you fall now -
For I'se still goin', honey,
I'se still climbin',
And life for me ain't been no crystal stair .

Langston Hughes
United States

Latch-key Child

I found him
sitting in the cold dark room
watching television
and stuffing himself with sweets.

'Why didn't you,' I asked,
'turn the light and fire on?'
He didn't answer.
Just fingered his cap, embarrassed.

And then I remembered
how I'd once waited in the dark -
thinking that if I kept still
so would the shadow on the window.

Vicki Feaver
Britain

Space for Both of Us

'Only men can go in space, Mummy'
you said.
We sat at table, making
Lego laser blasters
hyperspace zoomers
for fighting in minefields
full of dinosaurs.
'Rubbish!' I said
'There was Valentina something -
and What's-her-name, the American teacher...
though she didn't quite get ther e...
and there are more in training,
and anyway, why not?
I'm having a spacewoman.'
(firmly fixing a square yellow Lego brick
in place of the lost head of my

astronavigatrix)
'So there! And my spaceship
can smash your spaceship anytime!'
'OK, Mummy' you sighed,
resigned at such eccentricity
'You can have a woman if you want to.'
And then your little spaceship
through lightyears of authority
swooped down on mine
and smashed it back to bricks.

Sue Hasted
Britain

An Accident

The playground noise stilled.
A teacher ran to the spot
beneath the climbing frame
where Rawinda lay, motionless.
We crowded around, silent,
gazing at the trickle of blood
oozing its way onto the tar mac.
Red-faced, the teacher shouted,
'move back ... get out of the way!'
and carried Rawinda into school,
limbs floppy as a rag doll's,
a red gash on her black face.

Later we heard she was at home,
five stitches in her forehead.
After school that day
Jane and I stopped beside the frame
and stared at the dark stain
shaped like a map of Ireland.
'Doesn't look much like blood,'
muttered Jane. I shrugged,
and remember now how warm it was
that afternoon, the white clouds,
and how sunlight glinted
from the polished bars.

We took Rawinda's Get Well card
to her house. She was in bed,
quiet, propped up on pillows,
a white plaster on her dark skin.
Three days later
she was back at school,
her usual self, laughing,
twirling expertly on the bars,
wearing her plaster with pride,
covering for a week the scar
she would keep for ever,
memento of a July day at school.

Wes Magee
Britain

My Sister

My little sister died last night
In the hospital.
She was four days old.
Only four days old.
And when I saw her for the first
    time
I don't think I'd ever been as happy.
She was so small and crinkled
With big eyes and soft soft skin.
And a smile like a rainbow.
Her fingers were like tiny sticks
And her nails like little sea shells
And her hair like white feathers.
Now she's gone, and my mum can't
    stop crying,
And my dad stares at nothing.
I loved our baby.
I'll never forget her.

James Toohey, age 11

Rock, our Dog

He's dead now.
He was put to sleep last night.
I was sad,
But I did not cry.

It was not the same
Without him there
To prance and
Muzzle his head
Into my arms.

Today we were going
To bury him
In the garden.
I helped dig the hole,
And then ran off.

Nicholas Hadfield
Britain

That Special Sunday

Tis on a certain Sunday
A special time of year
Old soldiers from all Britain
Stand to attention here.
The noise is hushed in London
On this very special day,
Poppies on the Cenotaph
Red amidst the grey.
Two minutes' precious silence
As we think of those who fell
Who died for King and Country
In that other place called Hell.
And those legions of old soldiers
Like shadows march on by
And they hold their bodies proudly
And stare towards the sky.

Ian Stirland, age 14

Slave Dancer

The slave ship sails,
Cutting the water silently, surely.
Masts sway with the wind
And the sails puff and billow.
Creaking timbers, groaning hold
Full of the black cargo.
Crack! the whip cuts the skin
Of the slaves who dance
To the music of a boy's flute.

Adrian Tuplin, age 12

Silly Poems

Puffer Fish

My sister had a puffer fish
She caught it from the pier
An oily, slimy puffer fish,
It lasted for a year.
And if you took it by surprise
Or frightened it or swore,
It puffed till it was twice the size
That it had been before.

Alas, one day the puffer fish
Completely disappeared
While puss looked rather devilish
With whiskers oily-smeared
And none of us believed our eyes
When suddenly we saw
Our puss puff up to twice the size
That she had been before.

Doug MacLeod
Britain

The Irish Pig

'Twas an evening in November,
As I very well remember,
I was strolling down the street in drunken pride,
But my knees were all aflutter
So I landed in the gutter,
And a pig came up and lay down by my side.

Yes, I lay there in the gutter
Thinking thoughts I could not utter,
When a colleen passing by did softly say,
'Ye can tell a man that boozes
By the company he chooses.' -
At that, the pig got up and walked away!

Anonymous
Britain

Dear Teacher

Dear Sir,

I'm writing this letter to tell you
Why our Jason is away.
He looked so pale and poorly
When he got home yesterday.
His face became quite hairy
And his teeth grew sharp and white
And his ears got long and pointed,
He looked a sorry sight.
Then his eyes became quite bloodshot
And his nose all wet and black
And claws grew on his fingers
And bristles up his back.
The doctor when he saw him,
He had a nasty fright.
In all his years of medicine,
He'd never seen the like.
Of course it was unwise of him
To recommend the vet -
Our Jason's very sensitive,
He's not a household pet!
But I can understand the doctor
Running quickly from the room,
When Jason started howling
And pointing at the moon
And slavering and growling
And trying to bite his throat,
He hadn't time to open his bag
And write a doctor's note.
You'll understand, I'm certain,
Why our Jason is away
He looked so pale and poorly
When he got home yesterday.

                    Mrs W. Wolfe

Gervase Phinn
Britain

From 'K'shoo'

Whed your dose is code as barble,
Ad you sduffle all the day,
Ad your head id is behavig
Id a bost udbleased way;
Whed your ev'ry joid is achig
With a very paidful cramb,
Whed your throad is dry ad tiglish,
Ad your feed are code ad damb;
Whed your eyes are red ad rudding
With the dears that will cub oud;
You cad safely bake your bind ub
There is very liddle doubd.

You've got a code - a code -
Ad idfluedzal code;
You cahd tell how you caughd id,
But id's got a good firb hode.
Your face is whide, your eyes are pigk,
Your dose is red ad blue;
Ad you wish that you were -
Ah-Ah-Ah-h-Kish-SHOO-O-O!

C.J. Dennis

Night Starvation, or The Biter Bit

At night my Uncle Rufus
(Or so I've heard it said)
Would put his teeth into a glass
Of water by his bed.

At three o'clock one morning
He woke up with a cough,
And as he reached out for his teeth -
They bit his hand right off.

Carey Blyton
Britain

If you should meet a crocodile

If you should meet a crocodile
Don't take a stick and poke him;
Ignore the welcome in his smile
Be careful not to stroke him
For as he sleeps upon the Nile,
He thinner gets and thinner
And where'er you meet a crocodile
He's ready for his dinner.

Anonymous

Hi, Coconut

Coconut tree
so tall and high
when I look up at yuh
I got to wink up me eye.

Coconut tree
yuh coconut big
like football in the sky.
Drop down one for me nuh.

If only I could reach yuh
if only I could reach yuh
is sweet water and jelly
straight to me belly.

But right now coconut
yuh deh up so high
I can't reach yuh
I could only tell yuh,
Hi,

Hi, Coconut.

John Agard
Guyana/Britain

Index of Poets